Bible Story Bulletin Boards

Stories, Activities and Patterns

by Mary McMillan

illustrated by Veronica Terrill

Cover by Kathryn Hyndman

Shining Star Publications, Copyright © 1988
A Division of Good Apple, Inc.

ISBN No. 0-86653-430-X

Standardized Subject Code TA ac

Printing No. 9876543

**Shining Star Publications
A Division of Good Apple, Inc.
Box 299
Carthage, IL 62321-0299**

Unless otherwise indicated, the King James Version of the Bible was used in preparing the activities in this book.

To the Teacher/Parent

This bulletin board book was written for children ages five to eight. Each bulletin board display is accompanied by a learning table placed near the bulletin board.

Each bulletin board idea begins with a familiar Bible story followed by an objective, a skill objective, preparation, a diagram of the board, table activities, patterns and independent activities.

The best way to enlarge a pattern is to trace directly from the book onto a clear transparency and place on an overhead projector. Independent activities can be copied directly from the bulletin board book. Be sure the children understand the directions before beginning the projects. Remember, too, that the final outcome is not as important as the effort. Praise the effort as well as the results!

Scriptures are taken from the King James Version of the Bible and are included on every bulletin board.

The table activities correlate with the bulletin boards, but much of the information provided could be used in independent lessons.

Enjoy!

Dedication

For Sammy, Matt and Sidney

SS1828

Table of Contents

Shining Star Publications, Copyright © 1988, A Division of Good Apple, Inc.

SS1828

THE SUN, THE MOON AND THE STARS

In the beginning—the very beginning—God made Heaven and Earth. It was a great deal of work. God took six days to complete the job.

On the first day God said, "Let there be light." And there was light. God let the light shine for some time and then there was darkness. God named the light "day" and the darkness "night."

On the second day God made the sky above and the waters below.

On the third day God separated the waters from the dry land. And on the dry land God made the grass grow, plants bear seeds and trees produce fruit.

Now, on the fourth day God filled the sky with the sun, and the moon and the stars. The sun and the moon were made to shine down on the earth, to separate the day and the night; to cause the seasons on the earth, and to trace the days and years. The stars were made to give us comfort through the night.

On the fifth day God filled the waters with every kind of fish and the skies with every kind of bird. God told the fish and the birds to multiply and to fill the earth. And God was pleased.

On the sixth day God made all kinds of animals—wild animals, cattle and reptiles. Again God was pleased.

Then God decided to make a man to be the master over all he had created. And God made this man in his own likeness. God also made a wife for this man. And God told the man and his wife to multiply and to be masters over all the fish, and the birds and the animals. God observed all that he had made, and he was pleased.

Now that all was complete, God had finished his work. So on the seventh day God decided to rest. God blessed the seventh day and called it holy for the creation was done.

OBJECTIVE: God gave us THE SUN, THE MOON AND THE STARS to mark each day of our lives. The calendar puts those days in order. Let's learn to use the calendar—a gift from God.

PREPARATION: Cover the bulletin board with bright orange paper. Make letters with black construction paper and staple on, or write the letters on the board with a black marker. On a piece of 14" x 14" poster board, draw thirty-five squares, 2" x 2", leaving room at the top for the current month and the days of the week. Write in days of the week with black marker and laminate poster board to preserve. Cut out and glue small pieces of Velcro on each square and in the space for the name of the month. Copy, cut out and laminate squares of numbered days. Glue pieces of Velcro on back of squares and on strips with names of months. Place the Velcro so it will stick together. Be sure to copy extras of the sun, moon and the star to use as fillers on the calendar. Keep squares in a box nearby and add the appropriate square each day. See patterns on pages 7 and 8.

SS1828

THE SUN, THE MOON AND THE STARS

SEPTEMBER						
SUN	MON	TUES	WED	THUR	FRI	SAT
☀	🌙	1	2	3	4	5
6	7	8	9	10	11	12
13	14	15	16	17	18	19
20	21	22	23	24	25	26
27	28	29	30	★	☀	🌙

"... and let them be for signs, and for seasons, and for days, and years"
Genesis 1:14

TABLE ACTIVITIES: Copy two additional sets of squares and laminate. Keep squares on table in front of bulletin board for game play.

Game #1: Turn squares over so that only the back sides show. Have children take turns testing their memories by turning over a square and then turning over another to see if they match. If the pictures match, the student gets to keep the matching pair. If the pictures do not match the student turns the pictures face down. The winner is the one with the most cards.

Game #2: Laminate strips of poster board with a word from the animal vocabulary list written on each strip. Play another matching game by having students match the word to the appropriate picture square. Give points for the correct response. The student with the greatest number of points wins.

ADDITIONAL: Cover part of the table with wax paper and put out blocks of clay, rolling pin and cookie cutters in the shape of the sun, the moon and the stars. This clay play will develop the child's fine motor skills.

Shining Star Publications, Copyright © 1988, A Division of Good Apple, Inc.   SS1828

THE SUN, THE MOON AND THE STARS
(Bulletin Board and Table Activity Patterns)

SS1828

MORE SUN, MOON AND STARS
(Bulletin Board and Table Activity Patterns)

ANIMAL VOCABULARY LIST:

1. shark   2. duck   3. bear   4. turtle
5. snake   6. penguin   7. chicken   8. snail
9. seal   10. donkey   11. pig   12. elephant
13. tiger   14. frog   15. owl   16. alligator
17. kangaroo 18. monkey 19. rabbit 20. cat 21. mouse 22. dog 23. bat 24. lion
25. whale 26. bird 27. fish 28. turkey 29. sheep 30. cow 31. camel

SS1828

A RAINBOW PROMISE

When Noah was six-hundred-years old, the world was filled with wickedness. God was not pleased, so He decided to wash the earth clean by flooding it with great waters.

Now, Noah and his sons were faithful to the Lord, and because of this God warned Noah about the flood. Noah was instructed to build a huge ark, three stories high with many rooms. The ark was to have one window and a door built into its side. Noah obeyed the Lord, gathered his sons together and built the ark.

Then, God told Noah that he and his wife and his sons and their wives would enter the ark and be saved from the flood, and Noah was thankful for God's mercy.

God explained to Noah that he was to gather up two of every living creature on earth and that he was to fill the ark with these living things. When the flood ended, these creatures would be able to reproduce and fill the earth once again.

Others laughed and made fun of Noah and his sons, but the rains began just as the Lord had promised. For forty days and forty nights the rains fell upon the mighty earth. Even the mountains were covered by the great waters. When everything on earth had been flooded, God sent a strong wind to blow upon the waters, and slowly the earth began to dry. And finally, the huge ark came to rest on a mountaintop.

After some time, Noah opened the window and let a raven out to search for land, but the raven found none. Noah then released a dove and let it search. Hours later the dove returned. Noah waited seven days to try again for some sign of dry land.

Early in the morning Noah sent the dove out again. Hours passed, and finally the dove returned. This time the dove held an olive branch in its beak, and Noah knew that the waters would soon disappear. Noah waited seven more days and then sent the dove out again. This time the dove did not return, and Noah knew it was safe to leave the ark.

When Noah and his sons reached dry ground, they fell to their knees and thanked God for saving them from the great flood. God was pleased with Noah and his sons, and He promised that never again would He flood the earth with great waters. The Lord put a rainbow of many colors into the sky as a sign of the promise to never flood the earth again.

OBJECTIVE: Each time we see a rainbow in the sky, we are reminded of God's promise to never flood the earth again. A promise is forever!

PREPARATION: Cover board with blue paper. Have students make a rainbow large enough to arch across the board. This would be a good time to incorporate a lesson on the color wheel by including primary and secondary colors in the rainbow. (red, orange, yellow, green, blue, and violet) Enlarge Noah and the animal (see pages 12 and 13) patterns to fit board. Use brown paper to make the ark and a black permanent marker to write Bible verse across the ark.

SS1828

A RAINBOW PROMISE...

"I do set my bow in the cloud . . . ."

Genesis 9:13

TABLE ACTIVITIES: Make a copy of the following page for each student. Color the ark, Noah, and the animals. Cut out, following heavy dark lines. Fold up on - - - - - line and down on +++++ line. Slide slots of rectangles onto slots at bottom of ark to make the ark stand.

ADDITIONAL: Place paper, brushes and paints on table. Provide the three primary colors, red, yellow and blue. Have the children mix the secondary colors orange, green and violet. Let them experiment with mixing other colors.

SS1828

A RAINBOW PROMISE
(Table Activity Patterns)

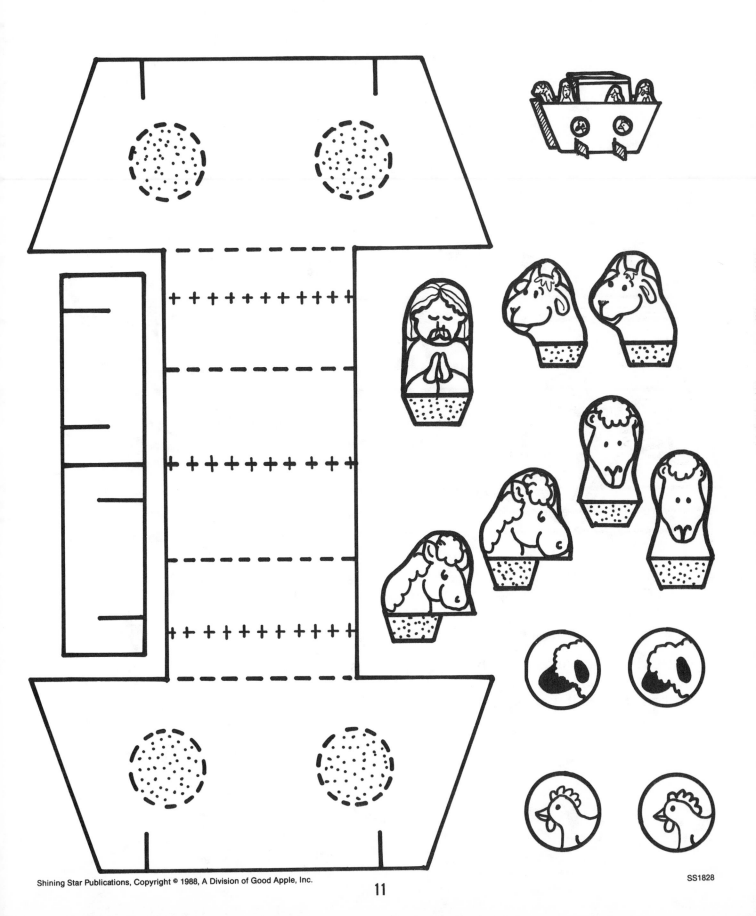

SS1828

A RAINBOW PROMISE
(Bulletin Board Patterns)

Cut one.

Cut two.

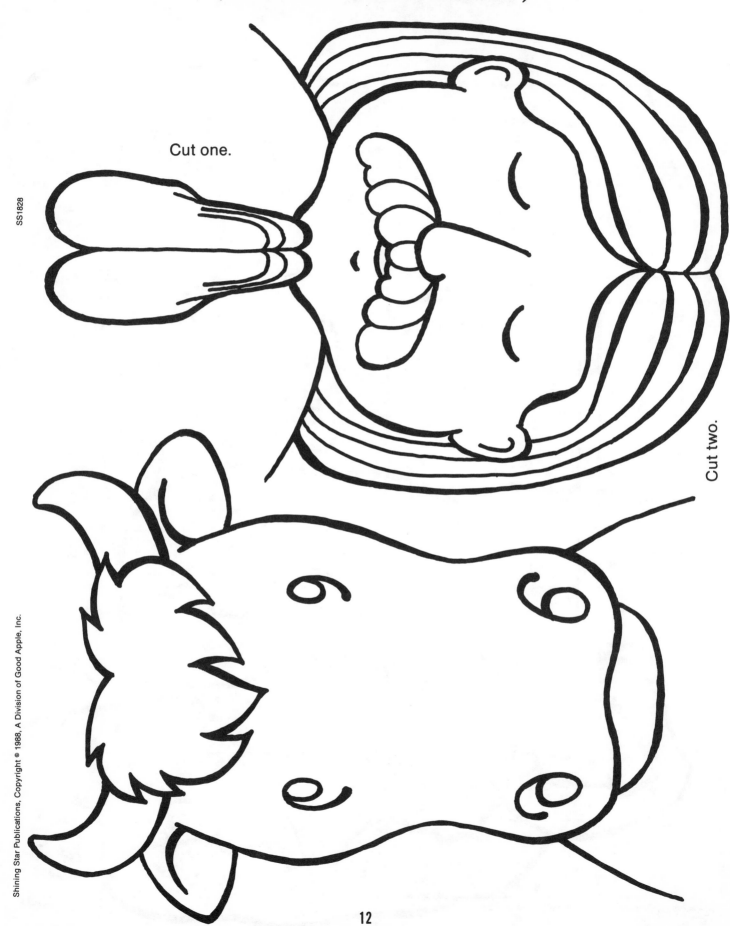

A RAINBOW PROMISE
(Bulletin Board Patterns)

Cut two.

Cut two.

SS1828

JOSEPH, THE DREAMER

Jacob had twelve sons, but Joseph was his favorite child. Jacob showed his love for Joseph by giving him a fine coat of many colors. The special attention that Jacob gave to Joseph made his brothers very jealous.

One night Joseph dreamed that he would become an important man some day and that his brothers would have to obey him. Joseph told his brothers about his dream, and they became very angry. The brothers were so jealous they decided to get rid of Joseph forever. The brothers grabbed Joseph and threw him into a deep well. As Joseph cried for help, the brothers discussed what they should do with him.

Shortly thereafter, a caravan of merchants and their camels passed by on their way to Egypt. The merchants offered to buy Joseph from the brothers. They could sell Joseph in Egypt as a slave. The jealous brothers were happy to sell Joseph for twenty pieces of silver.

As the brothers stood watching the caravan carrying their brother away from his homeland, they began to worry about what their father, Jacob, would do when he learned about their selfish act. The brothers plotted then to fool their father by pretending that some wild animal had killed Joseph. They took Joseph's beautiful coat of many colors, spread it with fresh goat's blood and gave it to Jacob.

Jacob mourned so for his beloved Joseph that the brothers were filled with sorrow for what they had done. Many years would pass, but forgiveness would come, and the brothers would obey Joseph, the dreamer.

OBJECTIVE: God has special plans for each of us. Sometimes those plans are told to us through our dreams. Joseph was a dreamer, and indeed, God had plans for him.

SKILL OBJECTIVE: The children will work with number words, numerals 1-12 and their values.

PREPARATION: Cover the board in brown or khaki burlap to represent the desert. Use bright colored poster board or heavy paper for the well. Draw squares to represent a rock or brick wall across front of well. Draw at least 24 to 30 squares—4" x 4" in dimension. Write the numerals 1-12, out of sequence, on the bricks or squares. Cut a small slot at the top of each numbered square, large enough for a paper clip to fit into.

Patterns for Joseph's head and hands, and for the water jugs are provided on page 16. Cut title letters out of the same color poster board or paper and fasten to board. Use a long strip of the same color poster board or paper; write Bible verse on strip with black marker, and fasten to board.

SS1828

JOSEPH, THE DREAMER

"... Behold, this dreamer cometh."   Genesis 37:19

TABLE ACTIVITIES: Cut out twenty-four 4" x 4" squares. On twelve of the cards, write number words—one through twelve. On the other twelve cards, draw dots—., .., ...,—through twelve. Have children match word or dot cards to numeral on board and paper clip together.

ADDITIONAL: Place several round oatmeal boxes on table. Cover with construction paper, and make to look like a well by drawing squares on box to represent bricks. Make the paper doll, Joseph and the colored coat, page 17, for each child. Color and cut out game. Use oatmeal boxes for props in acting out story of Joseph.

ALTERNATIVE STORYTELLING ACTIVITY: See pages 18, 19 and 20 for Joseph paper puppets instructions and patterns.

SS1828

JOSEPH, THE DREAMER
(Bulletin Board Patterns)

Joseph's fingers

JOSEPH, THE DREAMER
(Paper Doll Patterns)

SS1828

JOSEPH PAPER PUPPETS

Make your own paper puppets. Select clothes for Joseph, Jacob and two of Joseph's brothers. Also, put together one camel and two sheep.

1. Color.
2. Cut.
3. Put together with brads.
4. Cut out ten cardboard handles using pattern provided.
5. Punch one small hole in top of each puppet and two holes through each end of cardboard handles. Run string through puppet and attach to handle.
6. HAVE FUN! Act out story of JOSEPH, THE DREAMER.

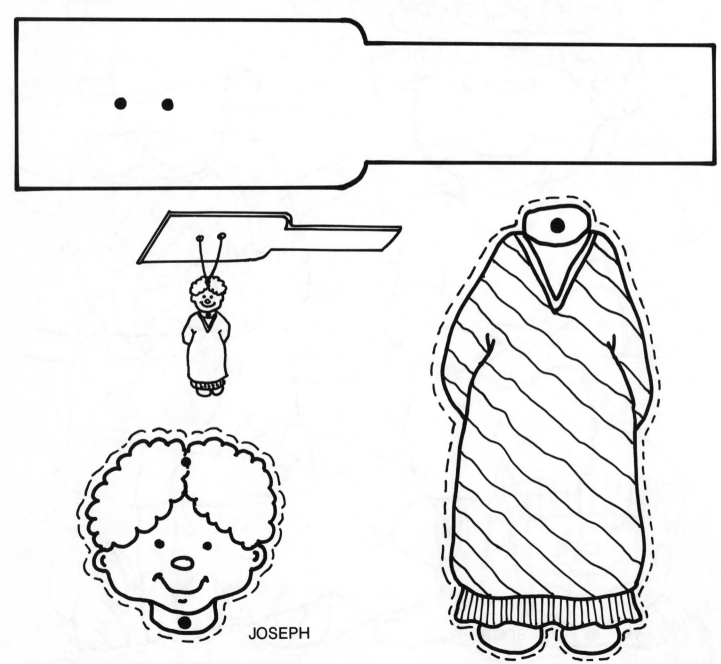

JOSEPH

SS1828

JOSEPH PAPER PUPPETS
(cont'd.)

BROTHER

JACOB

BROTHER

SS1828

JOSEPH PAPER PUPPETS
(cont'd.)

SS1828

MOSES—THE SHEPHERD

When Moses was grown he quickly realized that he was Hebrew instead of Egyptian, even though the Egyptian pharoah's daughter had raised him as her own child. Because he helped a poor Hebrew slave who was being beaten by the pharoah's guards, Moses had to flee for his life into the wilderness.

Moses traveled to a land called Midian, and it was there that he married and became a shepherd. One day Moses took his flock of sheep to graze near Mount Sinai. As the flock grazed, Moses noticed a burning bush. He approached the bush and saw that even though flames came from it, the bush itself was not being destroyed. Moses watched in amazement. Suddenly, the voice of God spoke to him from the bush.

God told Moses that the Hebrew people were unhappy in Egypt. He asked Moses to go to Egypt, gather the people together, and lead them out of the country toward a Promised Land where they would all be safe from the pharoah's guards.

At first, Moses was afraid because he did not think the people would believe that God had sent him. To prove that the people would believe, God instructed Moses to take the shepherd's staff which he held in his hand and to throw it on the ground. Moses obeyed and the staff was instantly turned into a snake. Moses knew that surely God was with him, so he took his wife and his children and set off toward Egypt.

It was not an easy task convincing the pharoah that he should let the Hebrew people leave with Moses. Time and again, Moses had to prove himself to the pharoah. Moses had to prove that God's power was stronger than the pharoah's power. Moses did this by bringing plagues and troubles upon the pharoah. There were plagues of frogs, of lice, of flies and even plagues of boils. Eventually, through these troublesome plagues, Moses convinced the pharoah to let the people go.

However, as Moses and the Hebrew people reached the banks of the Red Sea, the pharoah changed his mind and decided to stop Moses. After all, the pharoah was ruler over all Egypt, and he did not like anyone outsmarting him, not even God. But as the guards approached, once again God gave favor to Moses. God told Moses to stretch his hands over the great Red Sea waters. Moses obeyed, and as he did, the mighty waters rolled back and allowed the Hebrews to cross.

The pharoah learned that he was no match for God. He learned that his powers were nothing compared to the Lord that Moses loved and worshiped.

OBJECTIVE: Use this touch-and-feel bulletin board to teach the story of Moses leading the Hebrew people out of Egypt.

SKILL OBJECTIVE: These activities will make children more aware of their senses, specifically the senses of touch and smell.

PREPARATION: Cover board in blue paper for sky. Add green burlap for rough touch of grass. Cover lamb with cotton, for a soft touch, and spell out title with brown pipe cleaners, for a fuzzy touch. (See pattern on page 23.)

SS1828

MOSES — THE SHEPHERD

"Now Moses kept the flock . . . ."   Exodus 3:1

TABLE ACTIVITIES: Make copies of the two sheets of the touch-and-feel booklet, pages 24 and 25, for every child. Have students color pages first. Then, provide suggested materials on each touch-and-feel page and have students cut and paste. Cut out booklet sheets and fold on dotted lines. Place pages 2 and 3 on top of pages 1 and 4. Staple along folded edge to make book. Have children write title, MOSES—THE SHEPHERD and their own name on front of each cover. Encourage the children to decorate the cover.

ADDITIONAL: Place balls of cotton in separate bowls. Flavor each cotton ball with a drop of various scented extracts. Suggested scents are vanilla, peppermint, chocolate, lemon and strawberry. Children should be able to recognize each of these by smell.

To add to the touch-and-smell booklets, let the children put a drop of extract on each page. Suggestions: page 1—drop of vanilla on cotton, page 2—drop of mint on leaf, page 3—drop of chocolate on burlap and page 4—drop of strawberry on cloth. (This activity might need supervision!)

SS1828

MOSES—THE SHEPHERD
(Bulletin Board Pattern)

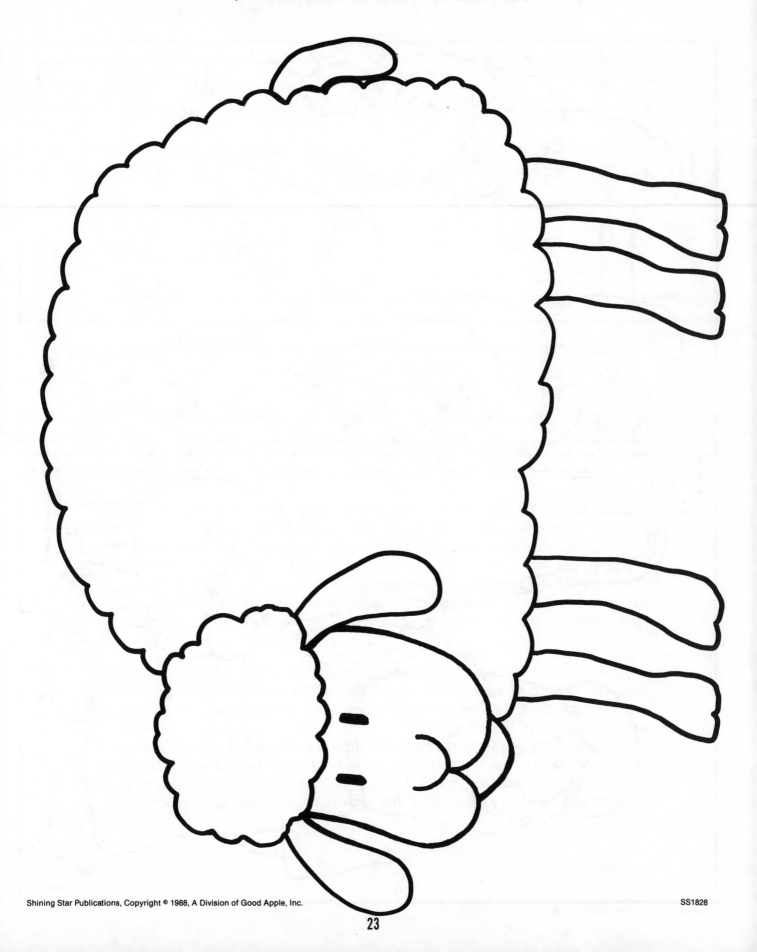

SS1828

MOSES—THE SHEPHERD
(Touch-and-Feel Booklet Pattern)

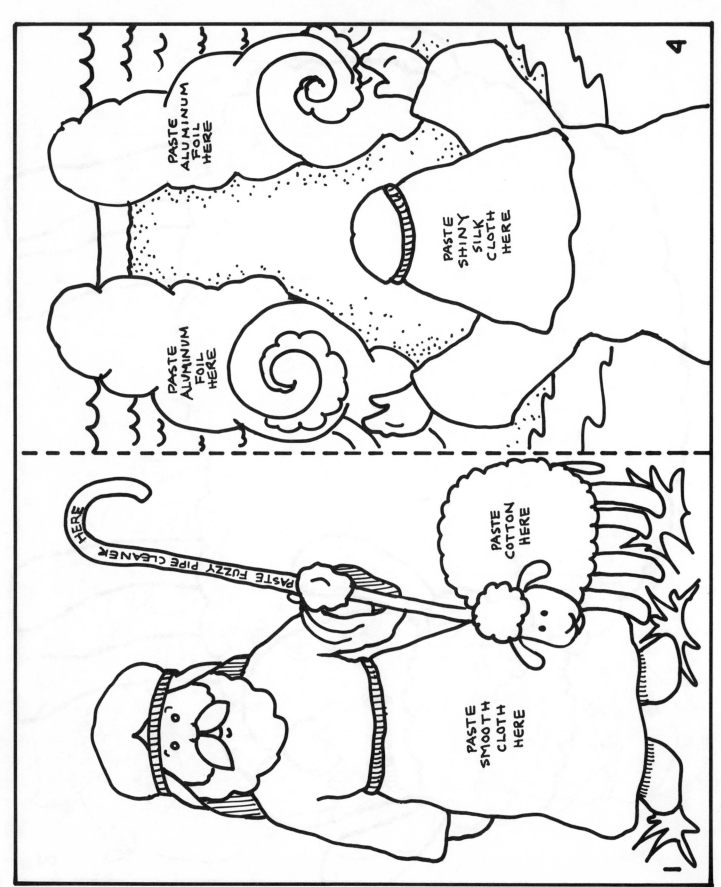

Shining Star Publications, Copyright © 1988, A Division of Good Apple, Inc.   SS1828

MOSES—THE SHEPHERD
(Touch-and-Feel Booklet Pattern)

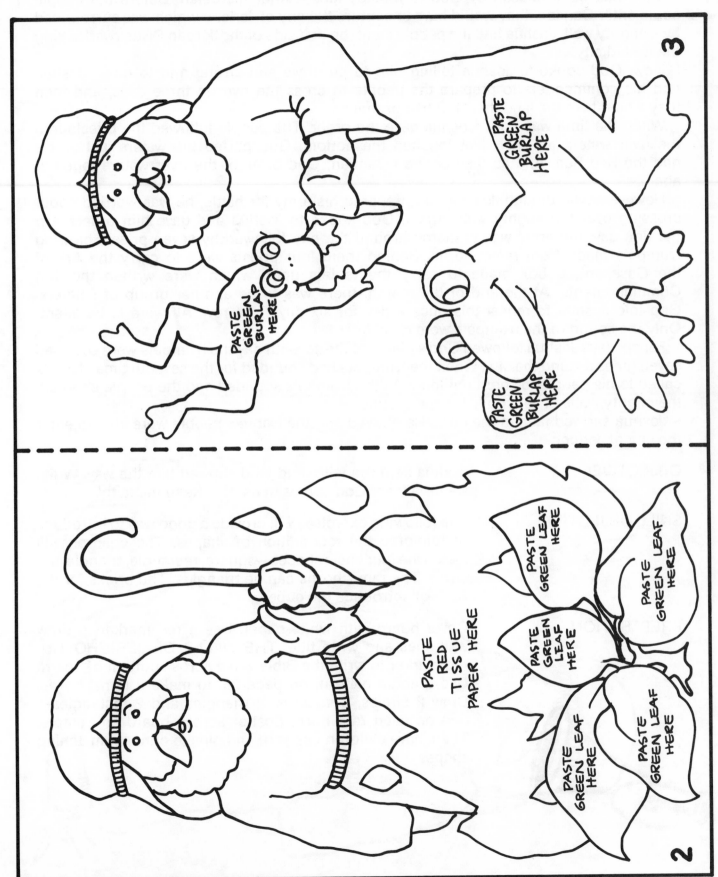

SS1828

THE WALLS OF JERICHO

Many years passed before the Hebrew people reached the promised land, Canaan. Joshua had been chosen by God to replace Moses after his death. Before the people could enter Canaan, they would have to capture the city of Jericho which was surrounded by a mighty wall. Joshua had the people camp on one side of the Jordan River, overlooking the walled city.

Now, God spoke to Joshua telling him to be brave and strong and to obey. Joshua told his commanders to prepare the people to cross the river in three days, and then they would take the land that God had promised.

When the time was right, Joshua gave the order. The people followed the priests into the river waters. As their feet touched the bottom, God parted the waters just as He had the Red Sea. And as they entered Canaan, God brought the river waters together again.

However, even though Joshua had prepared his army for battle, he was worried about crossing over the mighty wall. Again, God spoke to Joshua and gave him orders. On the first day, the army was to march around the city followed by seven priests blowing trumpets made from rams' horns. Behind them four priests were to carry the Ark of the Covenant, a box made to carry the tablets upon which were written the Ten Commandments. At the end of the march, there was to be another group of soldiers. God told Joshua to repeat this once a day for six days in a row. All were to be silent. Only the sound of the trumpets were to be heard.

For six days Joshua followed God's plan. On the seventh day the trumpets were sounded seven times around the city. When the trumpets had sounded for the seventh time, Joshua called to his people to shout out loud. As the trumpets sounded and the people shouted, the mighty walls of Jericho fell to the ground.

Joshua showed faith in the Lord. He obeyed and the Hebrew people were able to enter the city of Jericho.

OBJECTIVE: Joshua kept the faith, and God showed him the way. When we have fears God can calm us, too. Keep the faith!

SKILL OBJECTIVE: The following exercises will provide a good way to introduce or reinforce the recognition of shapes. The children will match the four basic shapes—square, rectangle, triangle and circle. The rams' horns can be triangles. The bricks for the wall will introduce the cube.

PREPARATION: Cover board with white paper. Use a red marker to draw wall lines and write title, THE WALLS OF JERICHO. Use red marker to write the Bible verse across bottom of board. Use triangle pattern, on page 28, to make 8 rams' horns. Draw 2 circles, 2 squares, 2 triangles and 2 rectangles—one on each ram horn. Scatter across board and staple. Then, have children use yarn and pins to connect matching shapes.

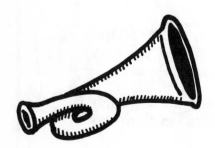

SS1828

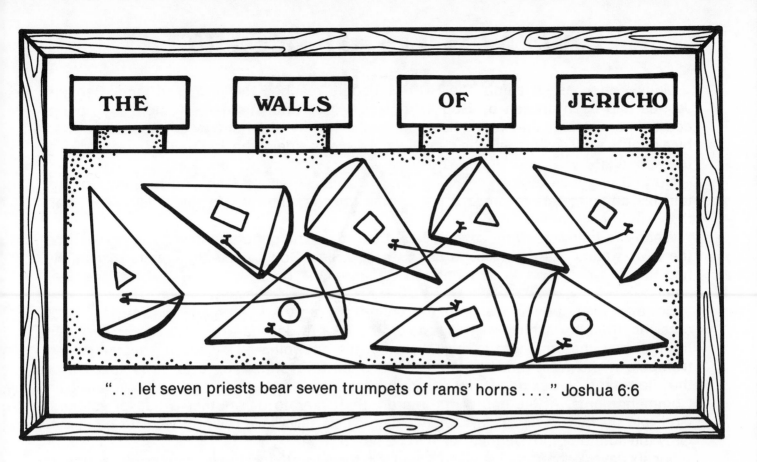

THE WALLS OF JERICHO

"... let seven priests bear seven trumpets of rams' horns ...." Joshua 6:6

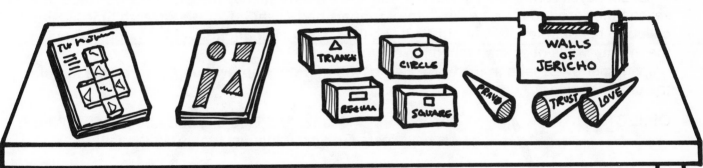

TABLE ACTIVITIES: Cut a large shoe box to represent Jericho. Print WALLS OF JERICHO across the front. Cut a piece of construction paper to look like the top of the wall and glue on the box top. Provide shapes of rams' horns for children. Have them write words of faith or draw pictures depicting faith, on the horns. Examples might be trust, love, honor, prayer, etc. Have the children place their horns in the box. At times, they may take their ideas out and share them with others.

ADDITIONAL: Put four small boxes on table. Paste one shape and/or shape word on the front of each box. Provide construction paper and scissors for children to cut out shapes and place in appropriate boxes.

ALSO: Make a copy of "WALLS OF JERICHO" pattern, page 29, for each child. Define cube. Children might want to stack their "bricks" to form the walls of Jericho.

SS1828

WALLS OF JERICHO
(Ram Horn Pattern)

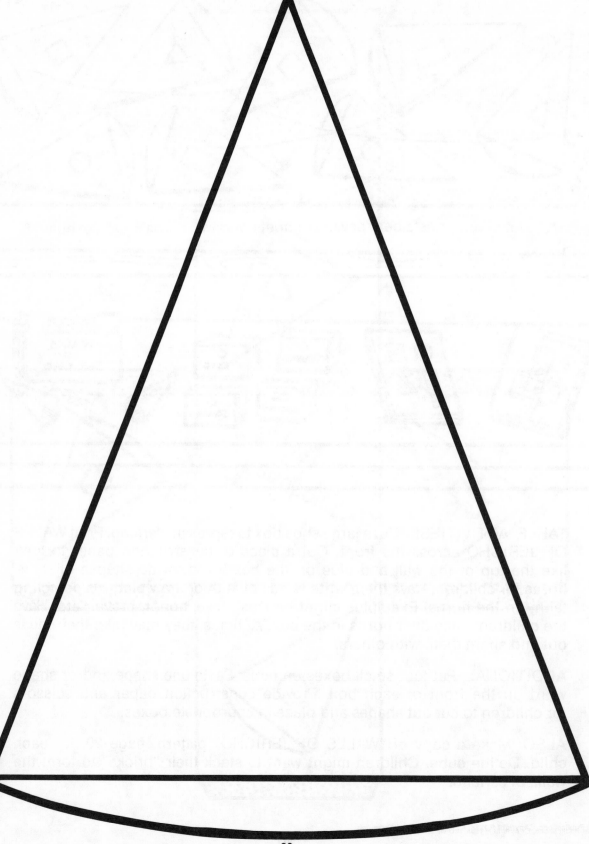

SS1828

WALLS OF JERICHO
(Brick for Wall of Jericho Pattern)

DEFINITION—CUBE: A cube is a solid with six equal square sides.

1. 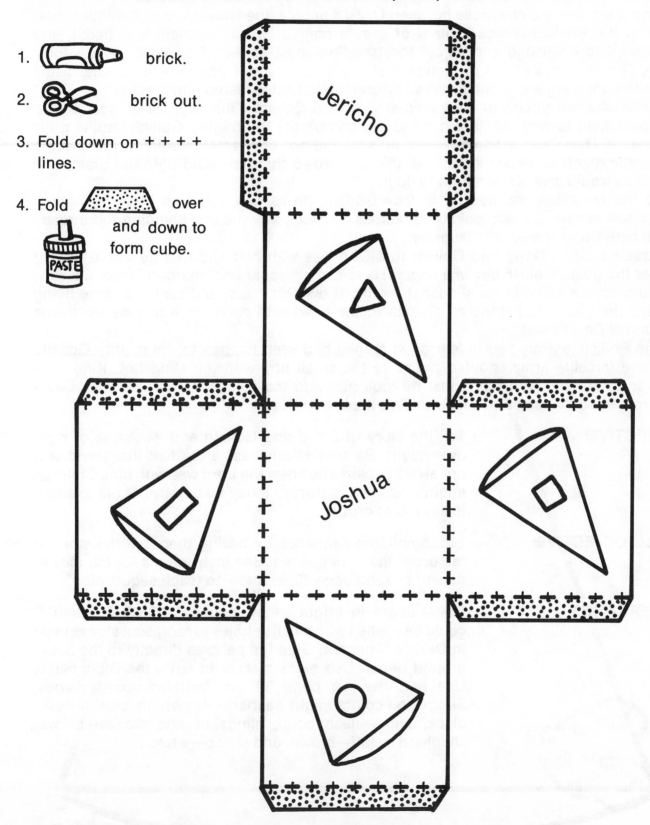 brick.

2. brick out.

3. Fold down on + + + + lines.

4. Fold over and down to form cube.

Jericho

Joshua

SS1828

DAVID AND GOLIATH

In the days of King Saul, there was a young shepherd boy who was loved and favored by the king. The boy was David who was also a musician. David was called to the king's court whenever Saul was troubled over his kingdom. David would play his harp and sing, and the music would calm King Saul and help him forget his troubles.

One day a fierce battle arose between David's people, the Israelites and the Philistines. Among the Philistines was a giant of a man named Goliath. Goliath was fierce, and he vowed to challenge and defeat the Israelites' best soldier. Day after day for forty days, Goliath repeated his challenge. But day after day, not one Israelite soldier came forth to fight the giant. Goliath was so strong the Israelites feared him greatly.

David was too young to be a soldier like his brothers. One day, David went out to the battlefield to visit. As he arrived, David could hear the mighty Goliath shouting his challenge. David was ashamed when he saw that not one Israelite soldier would stand up to the giant; so he spoke up and told the crowd that he would fight the giant, and that God would give him strength to do it.

As the small boy stepped up to face Goliath, he carried with him only a slingshot and a few stones. Goliath looked out across the field, saw the boy standing there ready to do battle, and roared with laughter.

However, when David told Goliath that God was with him and that he would indeed defeat the giant, Goliath became angry. He raised his spear and charged David. Quickly, David placed a stone in his slingshot, swung it over his head, and sent the stone flying toward the giant. The stone hit Goliath in the head with such force that he fell to the ground at David's feet.

The Philistine army fled in fear of what they had seen happen to the mighty Goliath, and the Israelite army shouted praise to the small boy with the slingshot. King Saul was so impressed with David that he took him into the palace to live with him. David had reminded the Israelites that with God there is no fear.

OBJECTIVE: Tell the story of David and Goliath and its theme of right over might. Be sure to emphasize the fact that David was not afraid because he knew the Lord was with him. Children might relate to this story in today's world by not being afraid to say NO to drugs.

SKILL OBJECTIVE: Teach children sequence by having them tell the story in the order that it happened. See instructions for the movie-theater box, on page 33, as a tool to teach sequencing.

PREPARATION: Cover board in bright yellow paper. "SIGNS OF DAVID" could be spelled with small pebbles to represent stones used in David's slingshot. Glue the pebbles directly to the background paper. Use black marker to write the Bible verse. Use patterns, on page 32, for bulletin board pieces. Suggested colors might be: harp—brown, musical notes—black, hand—flesh color, slingshot and stones—brown, shepherd's staff—brown, and sheep—white.

SS1828

SIGNS OF DAVID

"... and the Spirit of the Lord came upon David ...." I Samuel 16:13

TABLE ACTIVITIES: Children love to make signs. Provide the materials needed: pencils, markers, watercolors, scissors, crayons, etc. Give each child a piece of poster board at least 14" x 18". Make "SIGNS OF DAVID" and post around the classroom. Example:

ADDITIONAL: Use the instructions, on page 33, for a movie-theater box. Teacher will have to make the box on her own, but the children can make the scroll. (See instructions for materials needed.)

SS1828

SIGNS OF DAVID
(Bulletin Board Patterns)

MOVIE-THEATER BOX
AND SCROLL

The Story of David and Goliath

Instructions for theater box:

1. Use a strong cardboard box about 20″ x 14″.

2. Cut away top, leaving only the bottom and sides.

3. Cut out rectangle from bottom, leaving a 2″ border.

4. Cut holes on both sides for two wooden dowels to fit through. (See diagram.)

5. To preserve you might cover the outside with a vinyl-like self-adhesive shelf paper.

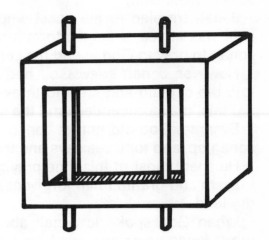

Instructions for scroll:

1. Provide a strip of white paper, long enough to make a movie scroll. Be sure strip is the right size to fit through the opening of box. Have the children divide the paper into sections and draw pictures of the story of David and Goliath in sequence. Using masking tape, fasten the beginning of the roll onto the dowel on the left side of the box. Roll the scroll onto the dowel and then tape the end to the other dowel. Roll the scroll back to its beginning, and the movie-theater box is ready.
Let the children use the box to tell the story in the order that it happened.

Note: This theater box will last a long time—if taken care of. Use it to tell other stories in your classroom.

SS1828

A WHALE OF A TIME

Jonah was a prophet and teacher. His job was to preach the word of God.

One day God asked Jonah to go to the city of Nineveh. The people of Nineveh had been wicked, and God wanted Jonah to speak to them and to tell them to change their way of life.

Jonah usually obeyed the Lord; but this time he was afraid, so he ran away and tried to hide from God.

Jonah traveled to the coast where he boarded a ship and set out to sea. While the ship was at sea, a fierce storm arose. The captain and crew were afraid. They begged Jonah to pray to God to end the storm.

However, Jonah knew God had sent the storm because he had not obeyed, and he told the captain and crew to throw him overboard to save themselves. When the sailors did this, the storm ended, and the ship was saved.

Even so, God did not let Jonah drown in the sea. God sent a large whale to swallow Jonah up, and for three days and three nights, Jonah was trapped in the whale's stomach.

He spent most of this time praying to God to forgive him. And the Lord heard Jonah's prayers and granted him forgiveness. God commanded the whale to spit Jonah out onto dry land.

When God spoke to Jonah about going to Nineveh, Jonah obeyed and served his Lord. Jonah could not hide from God.

Jonah had had a whale of a time!

OBJECTIVE:

The story of Jonah and the whale is a delightful way to teach children the overall power of God. We cannot hide anything from God, but isn't it wonderful how forgiving He is?

Have children sit in a circle on the floor and think of ideas about love and forgiveness, using this story as a guide. What a great way to have a "whale of a time."

SKILL OBJECTIVE:

Use the theme, "A Whale of a Time," to teach the skill of telling time. The hands on the bulletin board should be moveable so the children can set times. An independent activity is also provided to help reinforce the skill.

PREPARATION:

Cover the board in black paper. Adjust patterns of the whales, starfish, Jonah and his hands, on pages 36 and 37, to the appropriate size for the bulletin board. Use a bright-colored florescent poster board for lettering A WHALE OF A TIME, and the whale and starfish patterns. Write numbers on whales, and Bible verse on the starfish, with black marker. Use tagboard for patterns of Jonah's head and hands. Color in hair, mustache and features with markers. For movable hands, use a large-head brad to attach hands securely to Jonah where mark indicates. Staple parts in place on the bulletin board according to diagram.

(If possible, locate an old watch or an old clock for the children to take apart and actually see the parts inside. Hopefully, they will even be able to see the inside ticking.)

SS1828

A WHALE OF A TIME

TABLE ACTIVITIES: Make a copy of the JONAH CLOCK, on page 38, for each child. Color, paste parts onto tagboard, let dry, cut out parts and attach hands to face of clock with large-head brad. Children are ready to practice telling time. At first, work in groups with teacher. Later, work independently.

ADDITIONAL: Provide magazines and scissors so that children can find pictures of clocks and cut out. Watches, clock radios, grandfather clocks, sundials, fancy Swatches, VCR clocks, digital clocks, etc. should all be included. Have the children paste their pictures on colorful paper thumbtacked to the front of the table. Also, display clocks or watches on table for children to see and touch.

ALTERNATIVE ACTIVITY: See Jonah's flannel board folder instructions and patterns on pages 39 and 40.

SS1828

A WHALE OF A TIME
(Bulletin Board Patterns)

6

SS1828

MORE WHALE OF A TIME
(Bulletin Board Patterns)

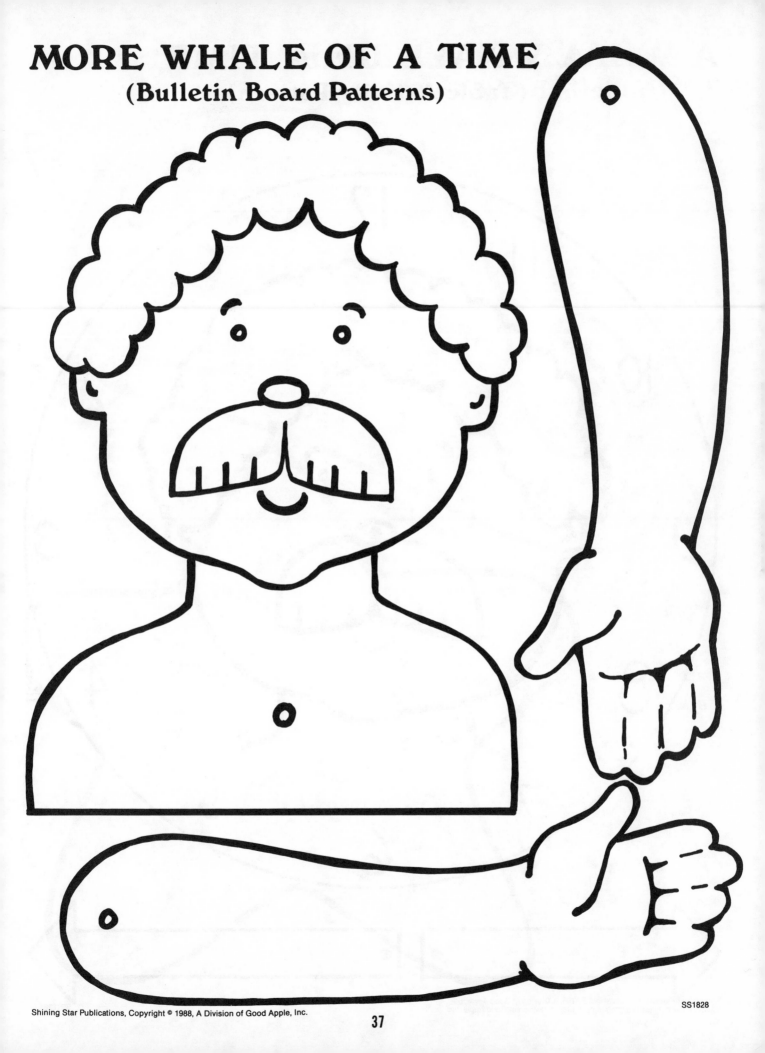

SS1828

A WHALE OF A TIME
(Table Activity Pattern)

SS1828

JONAH'S FLANNEL BOARD FOLDER

1. Give each child a plain manila folder and access to a stapler.

2. Place a piece of blue flannel (same size as folder) across the front of the folder.

3. Staple flannel to folder, leaving an opening at the top to store flannel pieces.

4. Make enough copies of the flannel patterns for every child to have a set.

5. The flannel folder and the flannel pieces can be used in acting out the story of Jonah during extra time.

6. The flannel sets could be made as gifts for the children to share with friends.

(The suggested color for each flannel piece is written beside the pattern.)

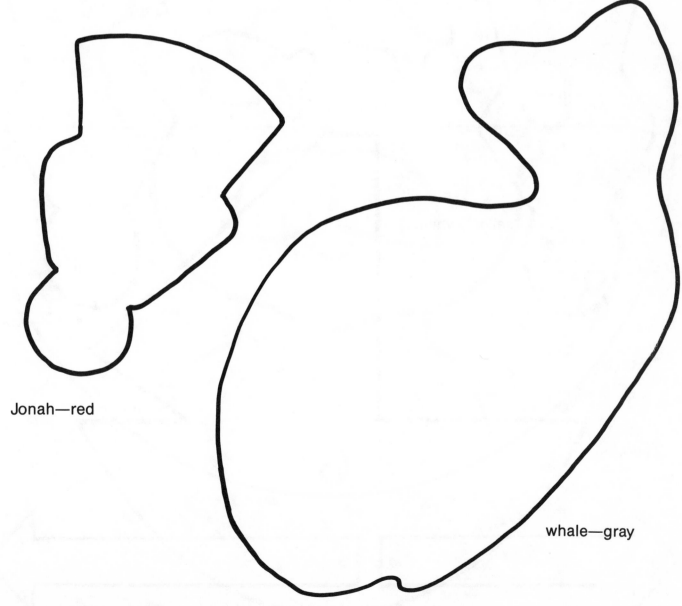

Jonah—red

whale—gray

SS1828

JONAH'S FLANNEL BOARD FOLDER
(cont'd.)

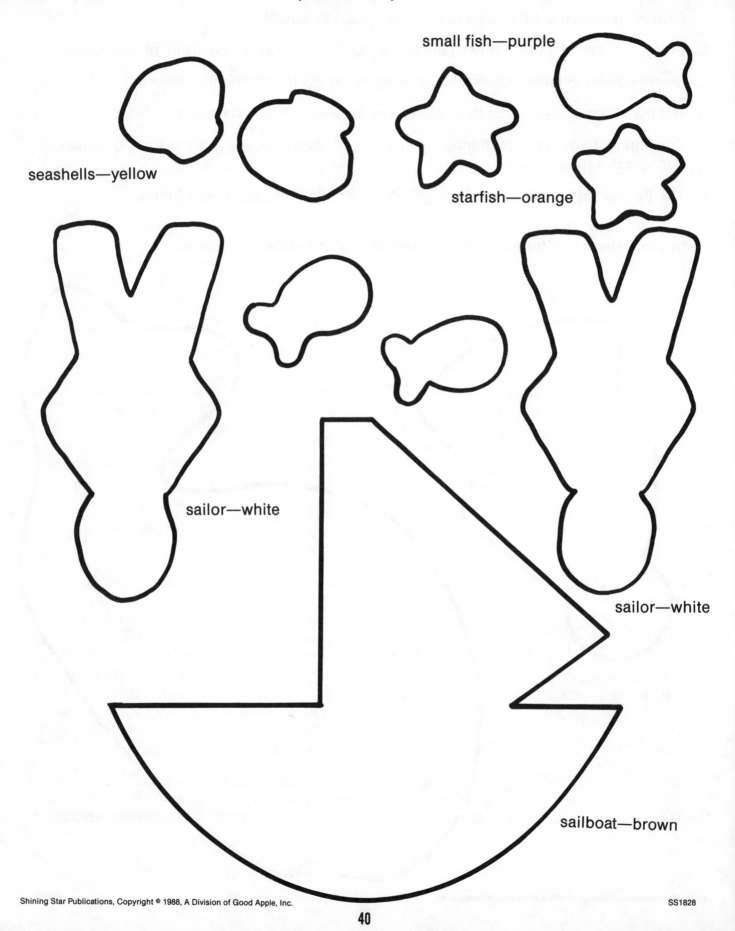

small fish—purple

seashells—yellow

starfish—orange

sailor—white

sailor—white

sailboat—brown

SS1828

DANIEL IN THE LIONS' DEN

Daniel was a wise and faithful man. Because of this, he was respected by King Darius. King Darius made Daniel chief president over all others. Daniel was favored by the king, and the other presidents became jealous.

Daniel's enemies knew that he prayed three times a day, and they decided to use Daniel's faith in God to displease the king. These men spoke up and asked the king to make a new law. The law would state that for thirty days no one was to show honor to anyone except King Darius himself. If anyone broke the law, they would be thrown into the lions' den.

King Darius liked this new law. He liked being treated with such respect. So he signed the paper, and it immediately became law over all the land.

Daniel heard about the new law, but Daniel was faithful to God, and God was much more important than King Darius. So Daniel continued to pray three times a day as he always had.

Daniel's enemies spied on him, and when they saw him praying, they ran to the king. King Darius did not want to hurt Daniel, but he had made the law, and he had no choice.

The king's guards arrested Daniel, threw him into the lions' den and rolled a huge stone across the opening to seal Daniel inside.

King Darius was not happy for he still respected Daniel. He hoped that Daniel's God would protect Daniel from death. The king could not sleep that night, and as soon as morning came, he rushed out to the lion's den and called out to Daniel.

To the king's joy, Daniel answered. God really had saved Daniel from the lions. King Darius was so happy that he ordered Daniel to be released and that all of his people were to respect the God of Daniel.

OBJECTIVE: The story of Daniel in the lion's den assures children that God delivers us from all kinds of trouble. This story teaches patience and faith in all things.

PREPARATION:

Cover board in black paper to represent lions' den. Enlarge pattern, on page 43, of lions' head, to fit the board. Make at least three or four heads. Use yellow, gold or light brown paper for faces and manes; or for a contrast, make the face brown and mane yellow, or the reverse. You might like to add long strips of curled paper around the mane to make it three-dimensional and full. Use any bright colored paper for Daniel's clothing and flesh-colored paper for hands and face. Lettering may be cut from paper the same color as lions' mane.

TABLE ACTIVITIES: Provide enough homemade salt dough, page 42, for each child to have an ample portion to make a lion. Follow recipe instructions for baking. After baking, let cool and then paint.

SS1828

DANIEL IN THE LIONS' DEN

"...he will deliver thee."

Daniel 6:16

SALT DOUGH RECIPE:

Ingredients—2 cups flour, 1 cup salt and 1 cup water

Combine flour and salt. Mix well. Add water a little at a time. Mix until ball is formed. Knead until smooth and firm.

Form into lion shapes. Bake in 325 degree oven—10 to 15 minutes or until hard. Cool. Paint or varnish.

ADDITIONAL: Enlarge the patterns on pages 45 and 46, 5 lions, 1 Daniel, 1 King Darius, 2 soldiers and 1 large rock on pieces of cardboard or heavy poster board—24" x 18". Have the characters carry the props, with their faces showing through cutout circles, and perform play on page 44. Take turns so everyone has a chance to act.

ALTERNATIVE STORYTELLING ACTIVITY: See Daniel's garden glove puppet instructions on page 47.

SS1828

DANIEL
(Bulletin Board Patterns)

SS1828

DANIEL IN THE LIONS' DEN

CHARACTERS:
Daniel
King Darius
2 soldiers
5 lions

PROP:
1 large rock

CURTAIN OPENS: *(Daniel is kneeling and praying to God.)*

KING DARIUS: Daniel, you have broken the law that says you are to pray only to me. *(Darius turns to call offstage.)* Soldiers, come!

SOLDIERS: *(Two soldiers enter.)* You called, O King?

KING DARIUS: Take Daniel at once and throw him into the lions' den.

SOLDIERS: *(The two soldiers throw Daniel into the den with five hungry lions.)*

KING DARIUS: Now, let's see if your God can deliver you from hungry lions!

SOLDIERS: *(The soldiers roll a heavy rock over the entrance and take their post on either side of the rock.)*

KING DARIUS: *(King Darius walks offstage.)*

FIVE HUNGRY LIONS: *(The hungry lions walk around Daniel, one at a time, licking their chops. As each one leans to sniff Daniel, he lovingly pats the lions on their mane. The lions become tame and docile. Daniel and the lions settle down for the night.)*

KING DARIUS: *(Returns the next morning.)* Soldiers roll back the stone. *(When the stone is rolled back, Darius speaks.)* Well, Daniel, was your God able to deliver you from the lions? *(King Darius laughs until he hears Daniel's voice. Then, the King shows surprise.)*

DANIEL: My God sent an angel, and the angel shut the lions' mouths. They have not hurt me. *(Daniel climbs out of the lions' den.)*

KING DARIUS: *(Falls down on his knees.)* Praise God!

DANIEL: Praise God, indeed.

LIONS: *(Roar!)*

Shining Star Publications, Copyright © 1988, A Division of Good Apple, Inc.

SS1828

DANIEL IN THE LIONS' DEN
(Play Character Patterns)

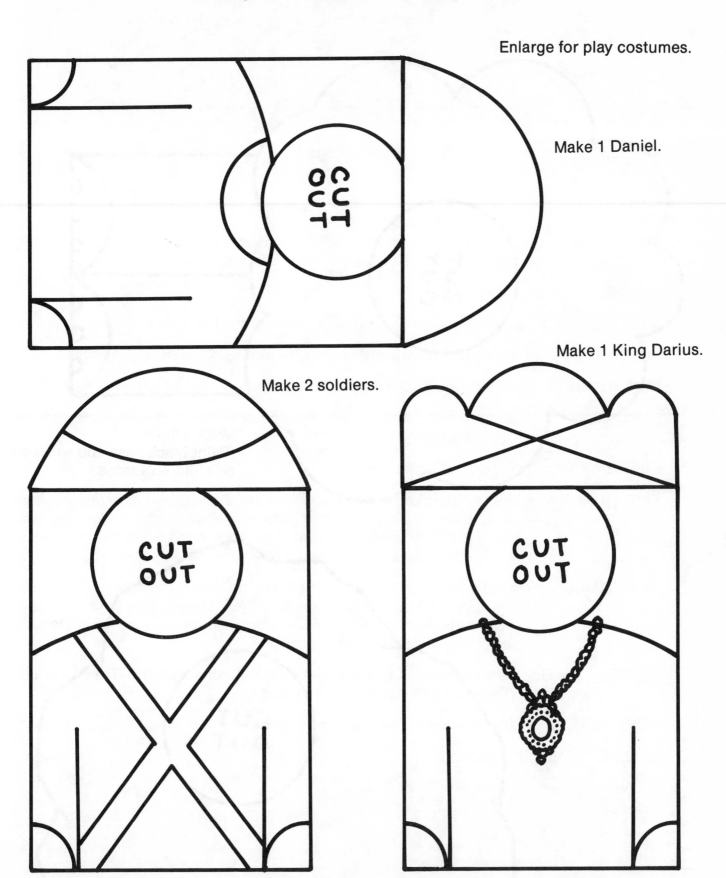

Enlarge for play costumes.

Make 1 Daniel.

Make 1 King Darius.

Make 2 soldiers.

CUT OUT

CUT OUT

CUT OUT

SS1828

DANIEL IN THE LIONS' DEN
(Play Character Patterns)

CUT OUT

Make 5 lions.
(Paint black nose and whiskers on children's faces.)

CUT OUT

SS1828

DANIEL'S GARDEN GLOVE PUPPETS

Have each child bring a garden glove to class. (Right for the right-handed and left for the left-handed.)

Provide 5 small chenille balls for each glove.
  1 pink for Daniel
  1 pink for King Darius
  3 yellow for the lions

Lions:
  Cut eyes and nose out of black construction paper and glue onto yellow chenille balls to make faces.

King Darius:
  Glue small paper crown on top of head which has been made from a pink chenille ball, and add 2 blue eyes and a red nose cut from construction paper.

Daniel:
  Color top of "head" with brown marker to represent hair. Add 2 blue eyes and a brown nose cut from construction paper to make face.

Glue decorated chenille balls onto the ends of each finger and thumb of garden glove and act out story of Daniel in the lions' den.

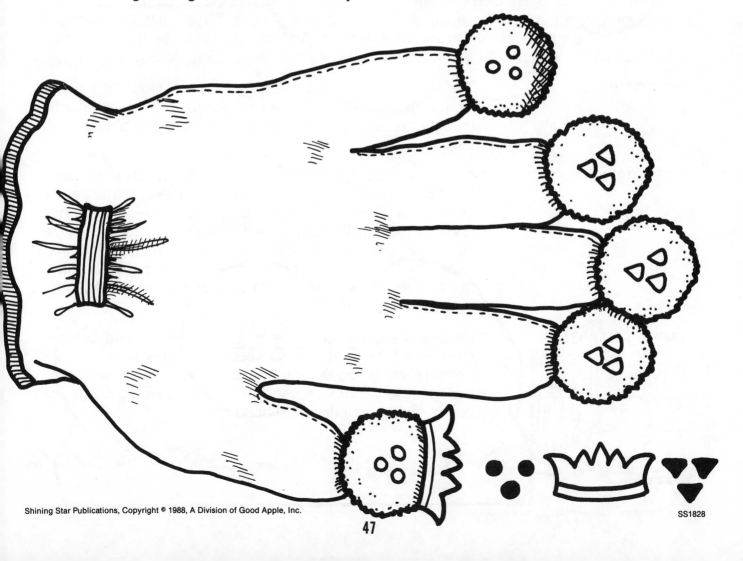

SS1828

THE BIRTH OF JESUS

In the days of King Herod, God sent an angel to earth. The angel appeared before a young woman named Mary. The angel told Mary she was favored by God; that she would have a child, and the child would be the Son of God. Mary was told to name the child Jesus.

Soon after, Mary married Joseph the carpenter, and they planned to care for Jesus and love him dearly.

Now after Mary and Joseph married, Caesar Augustus decided to take a count of all the people in his empire so he could tax them. Citizens had to return to the town where they were born, so Mary and Joseph made plans to travel to Bethlehem.

Joseph did not want Mary to travel because it was almost time for Mary to give birth to her child; but they had no choice. They had to obey the law.

As soon as they reached Bethlehem, it was time for Mary to have her baby. Joseph searched for a place to stay, but the town was so crowded there were no rooms to be had.

One innkeeper felt sorry for Joseph and Mary, and he offered them his stable. It was there, in that tiny stable, that Mary gave birth to the Son of God.

Nearby shepherds were watching over their sheep. Suddenly there was a bright light shining around them and they were afraid. An angel appeared and told them not to be afraid, that they had good news for them. A baby had been born in Bethlehem who was Christ the Lord. The angel told them they would find the baby in a manger. The shepherds hurried to Bethlehem and found the baby. They told everyone they saw what the angel of the Lord had said to them.

Wise men from the East saw a star and followed its brilliance. These wise men brought rich gifts and presented them to the Son of God. And all who saw the star knew that God's son had been born. All gave thanks and rejoiced—except King Herod!

OBJECTIVE:	The birth of Christ is a time of joy. This bulletin board and its activities give the children an opportunity to experience this joy and share it with others, just as Jesus shares with us.
PREPARATION:	Cover the board in a blue paper. (See patterns on page 50.) The hearts should be red. Make the stars of bright yellow or shiny, aluminum foil. The manger is brown and the hay is yellow. For a 3-D effect, glue pieces of hay onto the yellow paper. Use white paper for the baby's wrap and flesh-colored paper for the face. Use black marker for lettering, or form the title letters with pieces of hay, and glue directly onto background paper.
TABLE ACTIVITIES:	Make a Manger-in-a-box scene. Have each child bring a shoe box from home. Color outside of box with crayons or markers, or cover with construction paper, wrapping paper or self-adhesive paper. If you choose to cover the boxes, smaller children will need help.

SS1828

THE BIRTH OF JESUS

"He shall be great, and shall be called the Son of the Highest . . . ." Luke 1:32

TABLE ACTIVITIES: Fill the box with hay, dried grass, or colored artificial grass. Use the pattern provided on page 51 to make the manger and place in the center of the box.

Have the children color and cut out the characters on pages 51 and 52. Glue a Popsicle stick to the back of each character. Let dry. Group accordingly (example, Mary and Joseph, the shepherds, the three wise men, etc.) and glue around the inside of the box. Each character should be facing Baby Jesus. Now you have a Manger-in-a-box.

FOR ADDITIONAL ACTIVITIES refer to *BABY JESUS,* a Christian activity book with reproducible pages and stickers, published by Shining Star Publications.

ALTERNATIVE STORYTELLING ACTIVITY: See patterns for Christmas hats on pages 53 and 54.

TEACHER'S NOTE: You will need to explain to the children that the Bible does not indicate that the wise men came to the manger (Matthew 2:11 and 16) but since we have come to regard them so much a part of the Christmas story they are included here in the Manger-in-a-box.

SS1828

BIRTH OF JESUS
(Bulletin Board Patterns)

SS1828

BIRTH OF JESUS
(Table Activity Patterns)

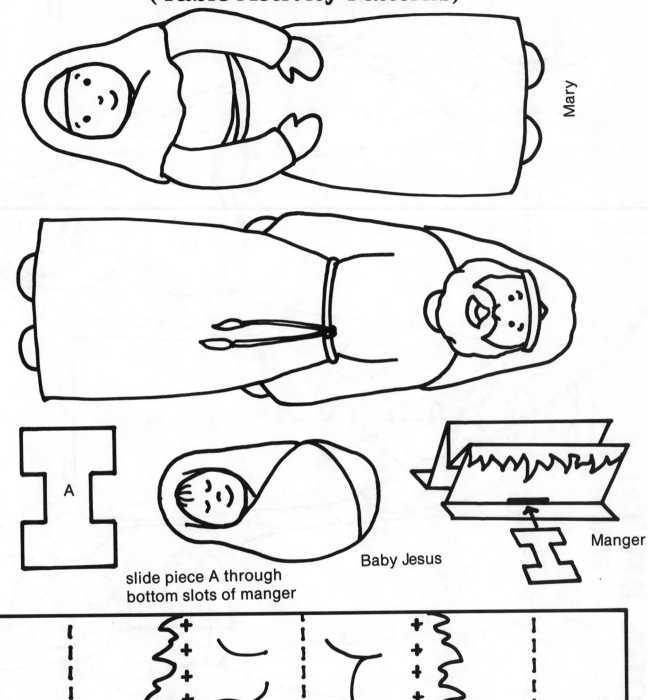

SS1828

Mary

Joseph

A

Baby Jesus

Manger

slide piece A through
bottom slots of manger

MORE BIRTH OF JESUS
(Table Activity Patterns)

Two Shepherds

Three Wise Men

SS1828

"HAT" FRAMES FOR ANY CHRISTMAS PLAY

Use the following pattern and instructions for "hats" for Mary, Joseph and the shepherds.

1. Take a long strip of poster board, 3" to 3½" wide and fit around head and staple ends together. (Be sure to use a child for a model.)

2. Cut out at least 2 sheets of tissue paper circles (for thickness) with a 1½" to 2" wider diameter than the headband.
   Fit tissue paper circles over headband frame and glue along inside frame.

3. Provide a piece of cloth (preferably cotton) 12" wide and 16" to 18" long. As you fit the cloth around the frame you might want to cut some of the cloth away to fit the headband.
   Glue along the top edge of the headband frame, near the tissue paper. Be sure to leave an opening for the face.

For Mary: Use pink tissue paper and pink cloth.

For Joseph: Use yellow tissue paper and yellow cloth.

For the Shepherds: Use brown (or white) tissue paper and brown cloth.

(This activity will require adult supervision. However, the completed hats can be stored and used year after year for Christmas plays.)

SS1828

"HAT" FRAMES FOR ANY CHRISTMAS PLAY
(cont'd.)

Use the following pattern and instructions for "hats" for the three wise men.

1. Enlarge the pattern provided on a long strip of poster board (use 3 colors if available) to fit around a child's head. Make 3 and staple ends together.

2. Decorate one crown by spreading glue and sprinkling on glitter.

3. Decorate the second crown by gluing on fake jewels or shiny stones.

4. Decorate the third crown by gluing on pieces of bright colored yarn or string.

5. Or—use your own imagination and decorate, decorate, decorate!

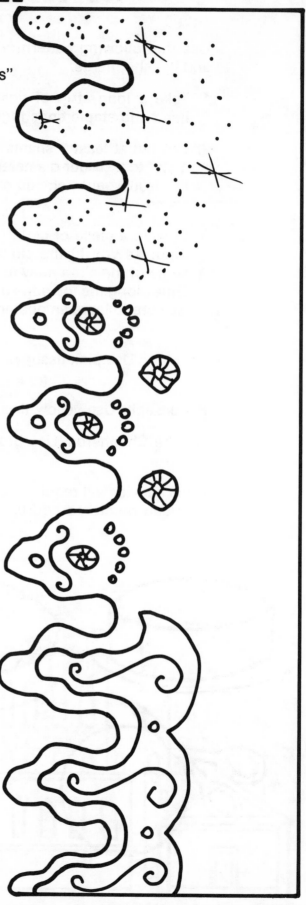

SS1828

HAVE YOU SEEN JESUS?

When Jesus was a boy, Joseph and Mary took Him to the city of Nazareth in Galilee to live. Joseph worked hard as a carpenter to support his family.

Joseph and Mary were faithful Jews. Every year they visited Jerusalem, the Holy City, for the Passover feast. When Jesus was twelve years old, he went with them.

The city was filled with excitement. Joseph and Mary allowed Jesus to move about the city among the crowds of people.

When the feast ended days later, Joseph and Mary started back to Nazareth with friends and relatives and it was discovered that Jesus was not among them. They hurried back to Jerusalem, and for three days they searched for Jesus. They were sick with worry, but at last, they found Jesus in the temple.

Jesus was talking with a group of religious wise men. These men were amazed that a young boy of twelve had such knowledge of God's teachings, and they all agreed that Jesus was indeed a special child.

Jesus was sorry that He had worried His parents, but He said to them, "Why didn't you know where to find me? Didn't you know that I would be here in my Father's house?"

Joseph and Mary thought about what Jesus had said to them, and they took their Son and returned home to Nazareth.

OBJECTIVE:	Joseph and Mary were good parents, and they loved Jesus very much. Jesus had not meant to worry them. However, in this story they were reminded that their Son was growing up and that He had been sent to earth to serve God. This bulletin board helps to remind us of the same things.
SKILL OBJECTIVE:	Students will work on map skills. This includes following directions, finding locations and determining direction.
PREPARATION:	Cover the bulletin board with red paper. Use pattern, on page 57, for temple and cut from gray paper. Include drawing of Jesus on the gray paper, outline with marker and color with crayons. Staple temple to red background. Then, cover square showing Jesus with pink cellophane paper. Reproduce patterns of Joseph and Mary on white paper. Outline with marker, and color with crayons. Staple to board. Use black marker on red paper for lettering.

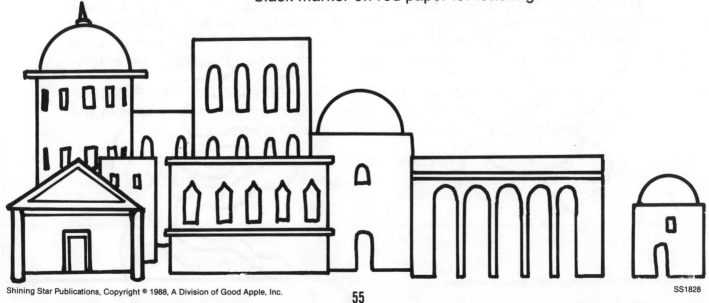

SS1828

HAVE YOU SEEN JESUS?

"... How is it that ye sought me? Wist ye not that I must be about my Father's business?"   Luke 2:49

TABLE ACTIVITIES: Make a copy of Jesus and the temple, page 58, for each child. Go over instructions with group, and then see if they can follow the instructions to make the temple. Be sure to provide all the materials needed: crayons, scissors, paste and sheets of clear cellophane to cover door. Upon completion, children should be able "to find" Jesus in the temple.

ADDITIONAL: Make a copy of HAVE YOU SEEN JESUS?—MAP STUDY, page 59, for each child. Smaller children will need the teacher to read the exercises. Have the children listen and follow directions.

ALTERNATIVE STORYTELLING ACTIVITY: See JESUS AND FAMILY-FINGER PUPPETS, instructions and patterns on pages 60 and 61.

SS1828

HAVE YOU SEEN JESUS?
(Bulletin Board Patterns)

SS1828

HAVE YOU SEEN JESUS?
(Table Activity Patterns)

SS1828

1. temple and Jesus.

2. out on _____.

3. Fold on _ _ _ _ _ line.

4. Jesus  to back wall inside temple.

5. clear cellophane over door opening from inside of temple.

6. Paste temple and roof on areas.

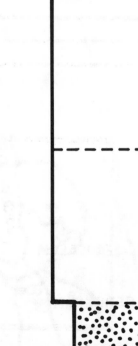

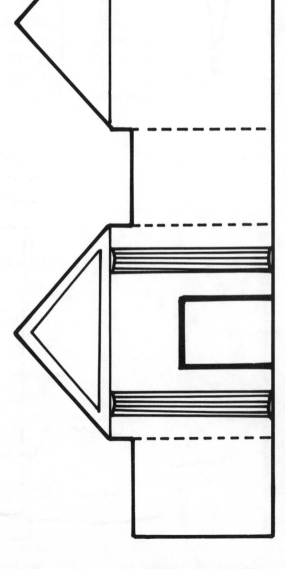

HAVE YOU SEEN JESUS?
Map Study

1. Jesus was born in Bethlehem. Place the star near Bethlehem.

2. Jesus lived as a boy in Nazareth. His father, Joseph, was a carpenter. Place the carpenter's saw near Nazareth.

3. Mary and Joseph took Jesus to Jerusalem when he was twelve years old. Jesus went to the temple to visit with the wise men there. Place the temple near Jerusalem.

4. The Dead Sea is near Jerusalem. The Dead Sea is salty. Place the block of salt on the Dead Sea.

5. The Mediterranean Sea is shown on the map. Place the fish in the Mediterranean Sea.

Look at the W—N—E—S symbol on your map, and answer the following questions.

1. Is Nazareth N or S of Jerusalem? _____
2. Is the Mediterranean Sea W or E of Nazareth? _____
3. Is Jerusalem N or S of Bethlehem? _____
4. Is Bethlehem N or S of Nazareth? _____
5. Is the Dead Sea E or W of Bethlehem? _____

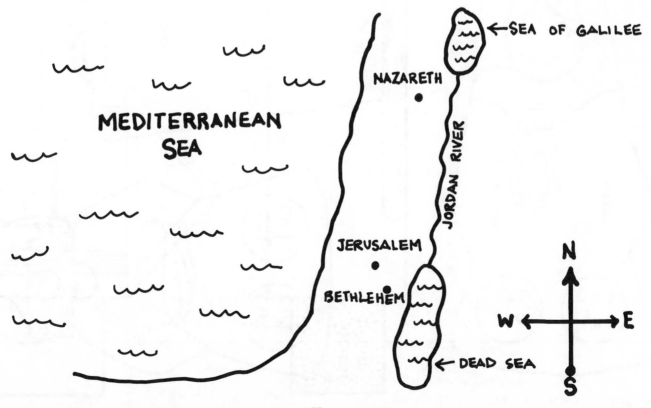

SS1828

JESUS AND FAMILY
Finger Puppets

1.

2.

3. Slide ▓▓▓ through | and glue tabs to back side of top section.

4. Slide first two fingers through ◯◯ to represent puppet's legs.

5. Act out story—HAVE YOU SEEN JESUS?

cut out

cut out

Mary

cut out

cut out

Jesus at twelve

SS1828

JESUS AND FAMILY
Finger Puppets

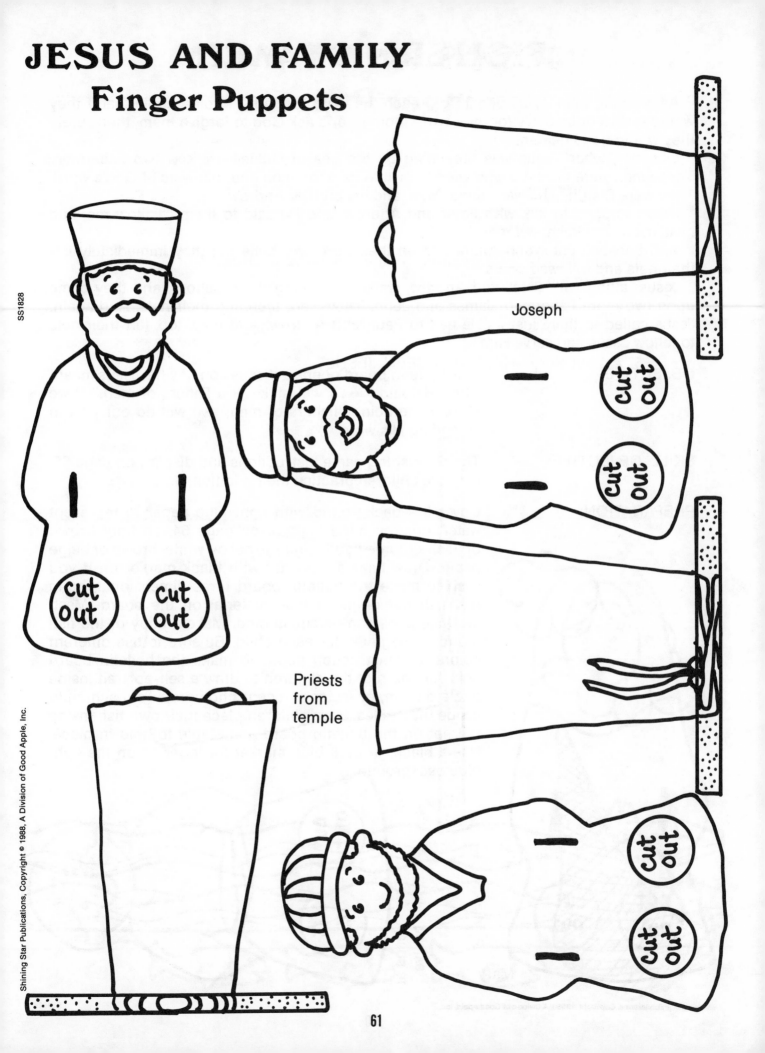

Joseph

Priests
from
temple

cut
out

cut
out

Cut
Out

Cut
Out

Cut
Out

Cut
Out

SS1828

Shining Star Publications, Copyright © 1988, A Division of Good Apple, Inc.

FISHERS OF MEN

As a young man Jesus began to preach the word of God. He told people that if they would repent or be sorry for their wrongdoings, and ask God to forgive them, then surely they would go to heaven.

One day, when Jesus was preaching by the Sea of Galilee, He saw two fishermen. These men were brothers who were known to be good men and followers of God's word. They were Simon, who was called Peter, and his brother Andrew.

Jesus stopped to talk with Peter and Andrew, and He said to them, "Follow me, and I will make you fishers of men."

And because Peter and Andrew loved their Lord and believed; they immediately left their nets and followed Jesus.

Jesus, along with Peter and Andrew, walked on along the seashore, and they came upon two more fishermen, James and John. They were mending their nets. And again, Jesus called to them just as He had to Peter and Andrew. And they, too, left their nets to follow Jesus and serve Him.

OBJECTIVE:	This bulletin board opens a discussion of what Jesus meant when He said ". . . I will make you fishers of men." If we all practice being "fishers of men," we will do our part in spreading His word.
SKILL OBJECTIVE:	The Go Fishing game instructions and display, on page 65, help the children practice their addition facts.
PREPARATION:	Cover the background with light blue paper to represent water. Enlarge hand pattern, on page 64, on light brown or flesh-colored paper. Enlarge net on white, brown or beige paper. Draw lines across net with black marker or, if you wish to make the bulletin board three-dimensional, hang real fish net or mesh type material on the board. Mesh produce bags can be substituted. Make a copy of the fish found on page 64, for each child. Be sure to use different colors of construction paper to make the bulletin board colorful. Instruct the children to draw a self-portrait inside circle on fish, or fasten a recent photograph of each child inside the circles. Have children place their own fish inside the net on the bulletin board and staple to hold in place. Use a black, or dark blue marker for lettering on the light blue background.

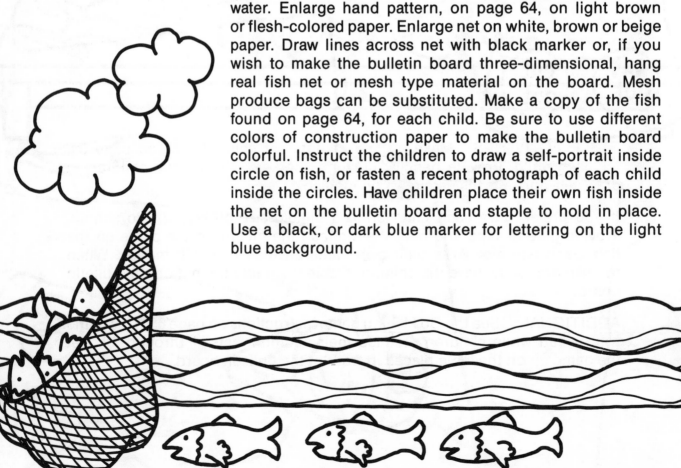

SS1828

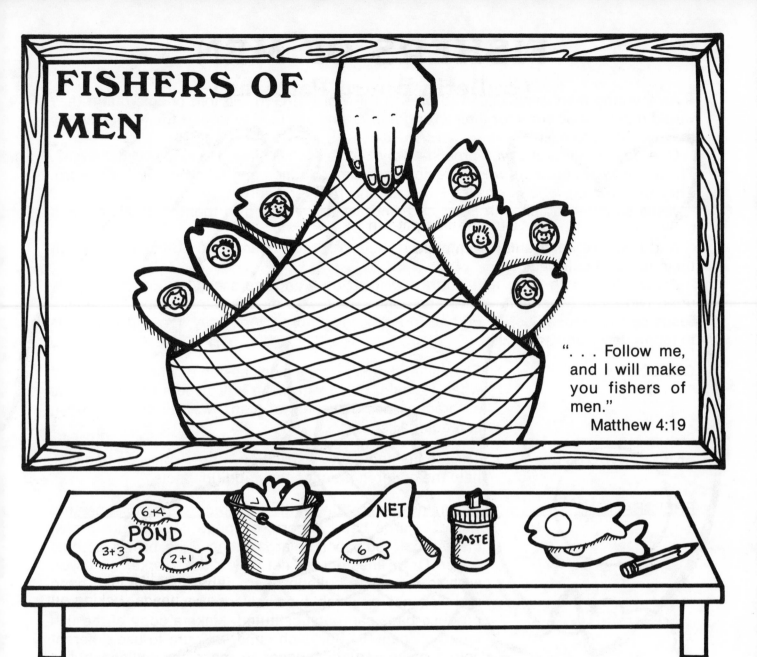

FISHERS OF MEN

". . . Follow me, and I will make you fishers of men."
Matthew 4:19

TABLE ACTIVITIES: Make a copy of different colored fish, on page 64, for each child. Provide pencils, crayons, markers, etc. for the children to draw self-portraits inside circles on the fish.

If you prefer, have each child bring a billfold-size photograph to school. Provide glue or tape and have them attach the picture to the circle on the fish. Each one may write their own name on their fish with marker. When the fish are ready, have the children staple them into the net on the bulletin board.

ADDITIONAL: See the Go Fishing game instructions on page 65. This game will be fun while children practice their addition facts, 1 through 12. Set the game up on the table placed in front of the bulletin board.

SS1828

FISHERS OF MEN
(Bulletin Board Patterns)

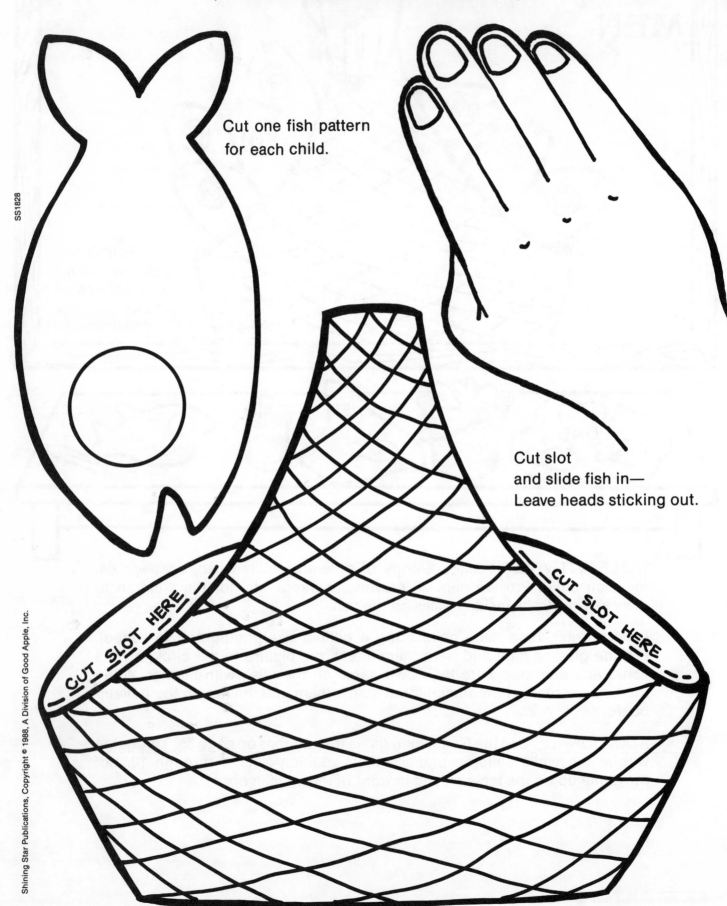

Cut one fish pattern for each child.

Cut slot
and slide fish in—
Leave heads sticking out.

CUT SLOT HERE

CUT SLOT HERE

GO FISHING
Game

Set up game according to diagram below. Use large piece of blue paper for POND and a large piece of brown paper for NET. Copy enough fish for addition facts 1-12. Fill the POND, with fish with addition facts written on them. (Example 2+3 3+4) Fill a bucket or can with fish with numerals 1 through 12 written on them. (Example 10 5) To play the game have children take turns. Draw one fish from the bucket. Select a fish with an addition fact that equals the numeral drawn. Paper clip the two fish together and place in the net. Have the children check each other as they play the game.

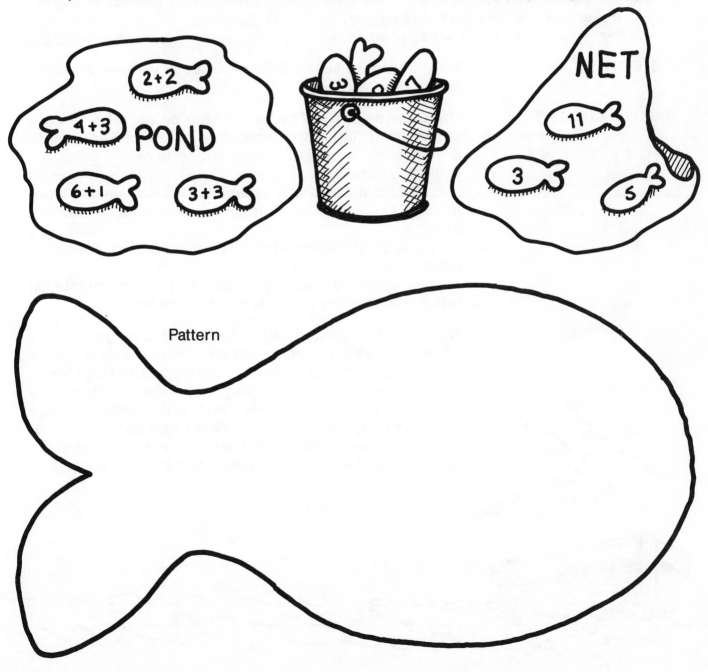

Pattern

SS1828

CALMING THE SEA

One day Jesus decided to cross the Sea of Galilee with His Twelve Apostles. Soon after they had begun to cross the sea in a small sailboat, Jesus fell asleep. He was tired from a long day of teaching and healing people.

Suddenly, a great storm came upon the sea, and the boat in which Jesus slept was tossed and turned. The waves crashed against the sides, and yet, Jesus was not awakened from his sleep.

The Twelve Apostles were afraid, and at last, they woke Jesus, and they cried out to Him for help, ". . . Master, carest thou not that we perish?"

And Jesus stood, and calmed the wind, and said facing the sea, "Peace, be still." And the winds stopped blowing, and the sea became calm.

And Jesus spoke to the apostles saying, "Why are ye so fearful? How is it that ye have no faith?"

And the Twelve were amazed, and they asked each other, "What manner of man is this, that even the wind and the sea obey him?"

And they believed, and they worshipped God.

OBJECTIVE:	". . . Why are ye so fearful? how is it that ye have no faith?" Mark 4:40
SKILL OBJECTIVE:	Use patterns of small boats provided on page 69. Cut out and laminate. Use a water-based, wipe-off marker to allow the boats to be reused. Some suggestions for using the laminated boats are 1) spelling words—for independent or group spelling word practice at table, or for putting the words into alphabetical order; 2) vocabulary words—for recognition and/or practicing definitions; 3) number words—for recognition, for putting in numerical order or for matching with number equivalent.
PREPARATION:	Cover the background with white paper. Enlarge the boat pattern, on page 68, on brown paper and staple in center of board. Enlarge the pattern for the waves and make three, two on blue paper and one on green. Staple all three onto board in place with the green wave in the center. Enlarge the pattern of Jesus on white paper and use crayons or markers to color. Then, place Jesus in the boat and place on the board. Use a blue or green marker for lettering.

SS1828

CALMING THE SEA

"...And the wind ceased, and there was a great calm."
Mark 4:39

TABLE ACTIVITIES: Place a large tin washtub-type container on the table. Tape a piece of paper on the side and label, Sea of Galilee. Then, fill washtub one-third full of water. Provide children with blocks of Styrofoam (or Ivory soap), toothpicks, paste and paper. Have children cut a small sail out of paper and paste it to side of toothpick. Stick toothpick into block of Styrofoam and launch the sailboat onto the Sea of Galilee.

ADDITIONAL: Patterns for small boats are provided on page 69. See instructions for using boats in SKILL OBJECTIVE on page 66. Have children work independently at table with laminated boats and markers. Boats can be used in various ways described in the instructions which include spelling words, vocabulary words, number words, etc. Use your imagination. Use and reuse the little boats for play and learning.

SS1828

CALMING THE SEA
(Bulletin Board Patterns)

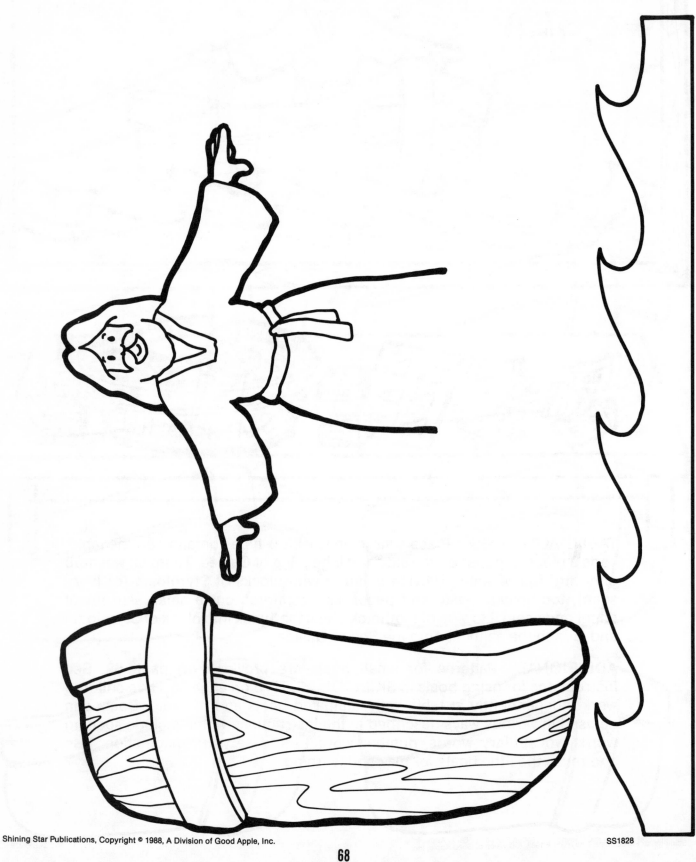

SS1828

CALMING THE SEA
(Bulletin Board Patterns)

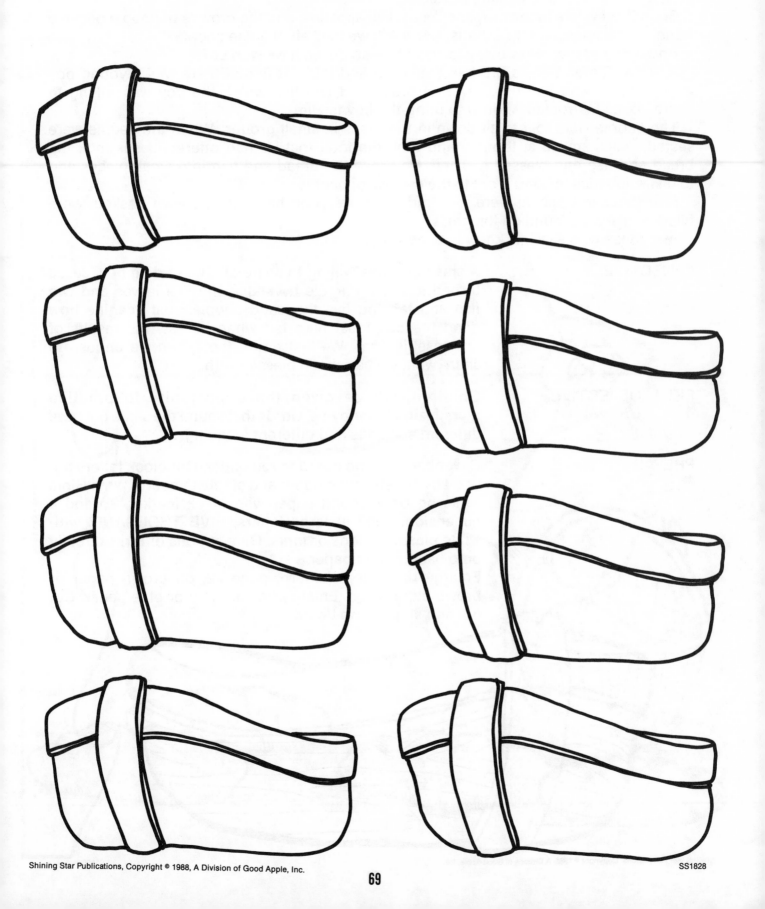

FEEDING FIVE THOUSAND

One day, Jesus crossed the Sea of Galilee and was greeted by thousands of people who had come to see Him. Jesus spent the entire day talking with these people, and preaching to them and healing the sick.

Soon it grew late in the day, and Jesus, His apostles, and the crowds of people became hungry. The apostles asked Jesus, "How will we feed all of these people?"

And Jesus asked, "How many loaves of bread do we have with us?"

Andrew, Simon Peter's brother, spoke up and told Jesus that there was a young boy in the crowd who had five loaves of bread and two fish which the boy was willing to share. Jesus instructed Andrew to bring the boy to Him.

The people were told to sit down in the grass in small groups. When the people were seated, Jesus smiled at the boy and took the food that He had offered. Jesus took the bread and fish and blessed it. Then, He broke the bread and fish into small pieces and told His apostles to hand it out to the crowds of people.

Five thousand people were fed, and after everyone had eaten; twelve baskets were filled with scraps found on the grass.

And those who saw this knew they had seen a miracle.

OBJECTIVE: A small boy was willing to share all the food he had. Jesus turned it into a miracle by taking the five loaves and two fish and feeding five thousand people. Just imagine how good the boy must have felt when he saw the results of his unselfish act. We feel good, too, when we choose to share what we have been blessed with.

SKILL OBJECTIVE: Children will be given the opportunity to practice recognizing homonyms, words that sound the same but have different spellings and different meanings.

PREPARATION: Cover background board in red paper. Cut block letters out of black construction paper and staple to board. Write Bible verse on background paper with black marker. To add a dimension, spell in large letters, FIVE THOUSAND, with white plastic spoons or forks. Glue spoons or forks directly onto background paper.

Enlarge bread loaf pattern, page 72, on brown paper or brown paper bags. Enlarge fish on gray or blue paper. Cut out and staple onto board.

Shining Star Publications, Copyright © 1988, A Division of Good Apple, Inc.

SS1828

WHEN JESUS

FEEDS FIVE THOUSAND!

"And they did all eat, and were filled." Mark 6:42

TABLE ACTIVITIES: Make a copy of FEEDING FIVE THOUSAND—HIDDEN PICTURE, page 73, for each child. Explain the instructions. Then, have the children find and circle the hidden parts, and color the picture.

Take time to discuss Jesus' feeding all five thousand people with only five loaves of bread and two fish! Act it out by bringing five small loaves of bread and two fish cakes to class. Be sure everyone in your class receives a small portion of each. Also, don't forget to bless the food, as Jesus did, by giving thanks to our Lord.

ADDITIONAL: Make a copy of FEEDING FIVE THOUSAND—HOMONYM REVIEW, page 74, for each child. First, explain the definition of a homonym and give some examples. Go over instructions at the top of the page. Let your class work independently, if possible. If the class is too young and needs help, do the page together.

ALTERNATIVE STORYTELLING ACTIVITY: See Feeding Five Thousand flannel board patterns and instructions on pages 75 and 76.

SS1828

FEEDING FIVE THOUSAND
(Bulletin Board Patterns)

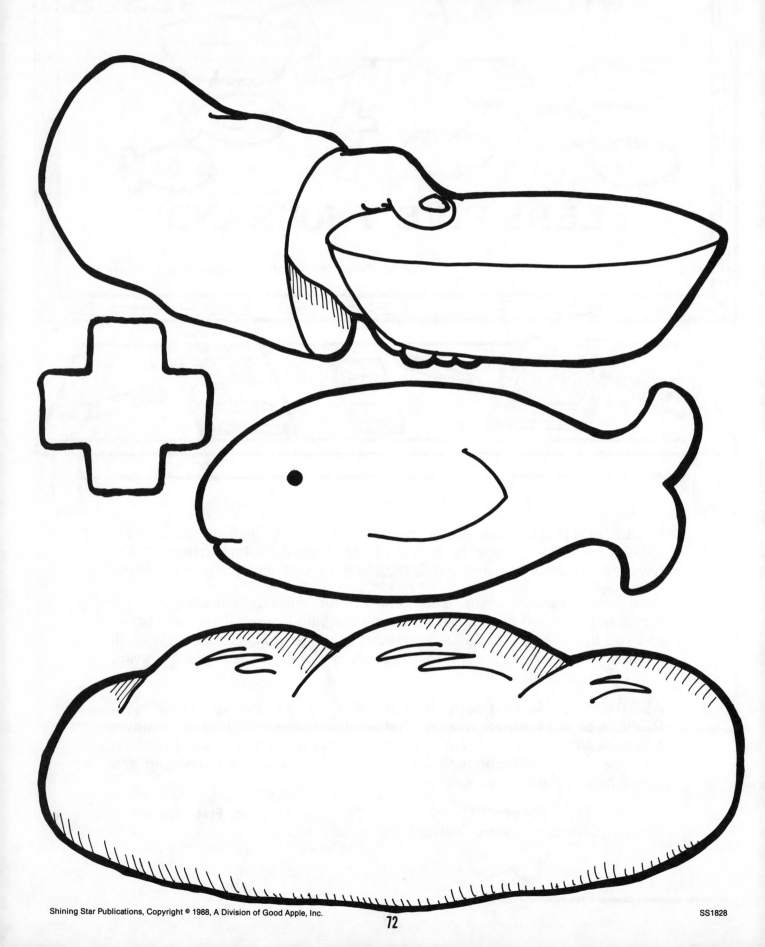

SS1828

FEEDING FIVE THOUSAND
(Hidden Pictures)

Circle 3 loaves of bread.

Circle 5 butterflies.

Circle 2 fish.

Circle 1 basket.

SS1828

FEEDING FIVE THOUSAND
Homonym Review

HOMONYMS sound the same, but have different spellings and different meanings. See if you can find the homonym from the list located at the bottom of the page for the bold-faced word in each sentence. Write the homonym in the blank provided.

a.

1. Jesus crossed the **sea** of Galilee. a. _____

b.

2. When Jesus reached the shore, he could **hear** and see crowds of people. b. _____

c.   d.   e.

3. The **deer**, and the **hare** and the **bear** watched the crowds from afar. c. _____

d. _____

e. _____

f.

4. When they became hungry, Jesus did **meet** a young boy who offered to share his food. f. _____

g.

5. The food was not for **sale**, so Jesus blessed it and gave it to the crowds of people. g. _____

h. i.   j.

6. They sat **right there** on the grass and **ate** with Jesus. h. _____

i. _____

j. _____

Choose one homonym for each blank:

meat	bare	they're
hair	write	sail
eight	here	dear
see		

See if you can match these homonyms by drawing a line from one to the other:

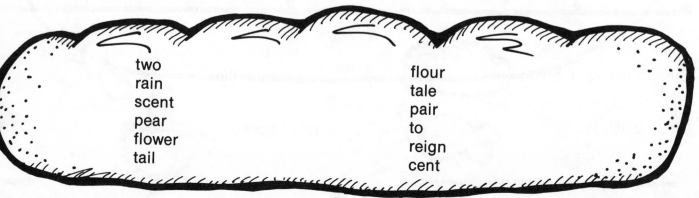

two	flour
rain	tale
scent	pair
pear	to
flower	reign
tail	cent

FEEDING FIVE THOUSAND
(Flannel Board Patterns)

Reproduce the following patterns on flannel cloth. Make 24 or more loaves of bread. Also, make five or more plus signs, and five or more equal signs.

Use a permanent black marker and write numerals 1 through 12 on 12 of the loaves of bread.

Have the children use the loaves of bread, plus signs and equal signs on a flannel-covered board to practice their addition facts.

Examples:

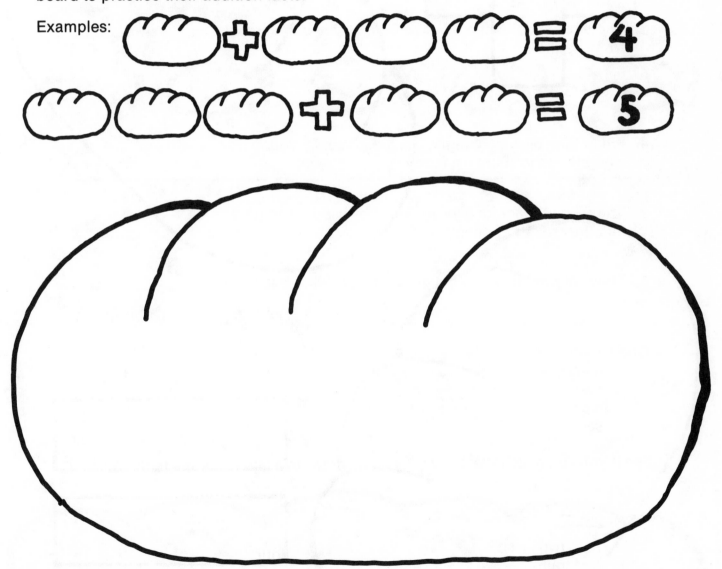

SS1828

FEEDING FIVE THOUSAND
(Flannel Board Patterns)

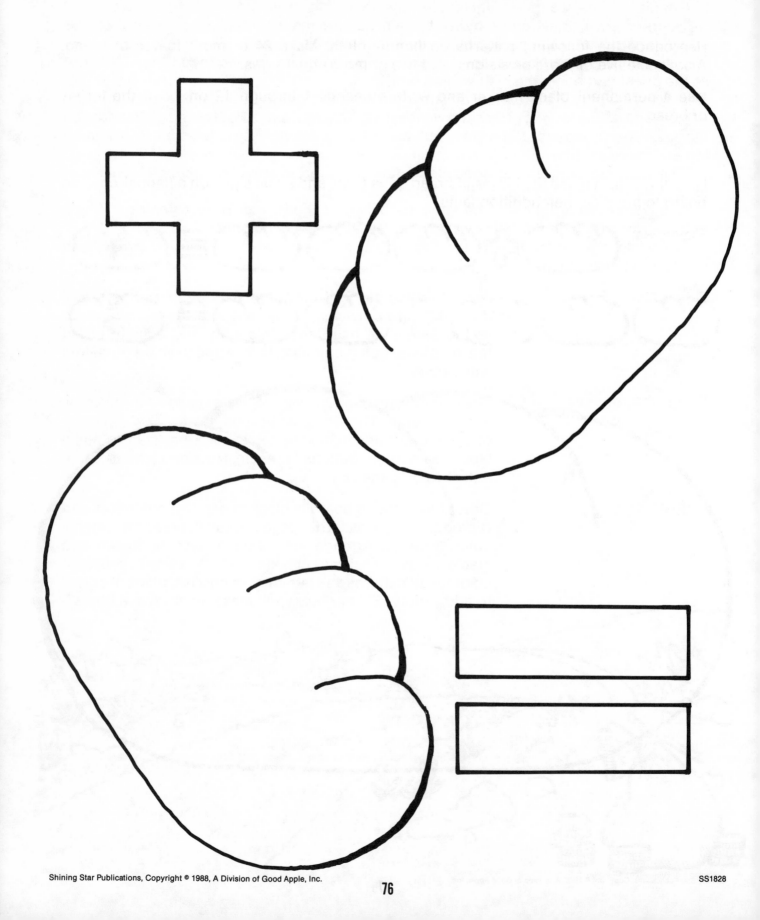

SS1828

THE GOOD SAMARITAN

Once when Jesus was teaching the ways of the Lord, He told this story.

"A man was traveling on the road from Jerusalem to Jericho when thieves stripped him of his clothes, wounded him and left him to die along the roadside.

"Hours later, a priest came by. But when he saw the wounded man, the priest was afraid to help him, so he passed by on the other side of the road.

"Later, another man came down the road. He, too, saw the wounded man. But just as the priest had done, the man walked on by.

"However, shortly thereafter, a Samaritan traveled down the same road. When the Samaritan saw the wounded man, he went to help him right away. He cleaned and bandaged the poor man's wounds. Then, he put the man on his donkey, took him to a nearby inn and cared for him.

"The next morning as the good Samaritan prepared to leave, he paid the innkeeper to care for the wounded man until he was better."

Now, when Jesus finished the story he asked of those who were listening, "Which of these three men do you think was a neighbor to the wounded man?"

Of course, they knew it was the Samaritan, and Jesus said to them, ". . . Go, and do thou likewise." Luke 10:37

OBJECTIVE:	Jesus told the story of the Good Samaritan and then told those who were listening to go out into the world and do as the Samaritan had done. This story and bulletin board teach us to be compassionate, to love and to share ourselves with others.
SKILL OBJECTIVE:	The patterns, on page 80, use two basic shapes—the triangle and the circle. The triangles fit together to form a picture of the Good Samaritan. The circles can be used to make Good Samaritan buttons. (See instructions under Table Activities on page 78.)
PREPARATION:	Cover background board in black paper. Cut out letters and reproduce hand patterns, page 79, on fluorescent, bright-colored paper. Arrange according to picture shown and staple to board. (You may choose to use the same fluorescent color for all patterns and lettering, or choose different colors to add variety. Either choice will make an attractive board.)

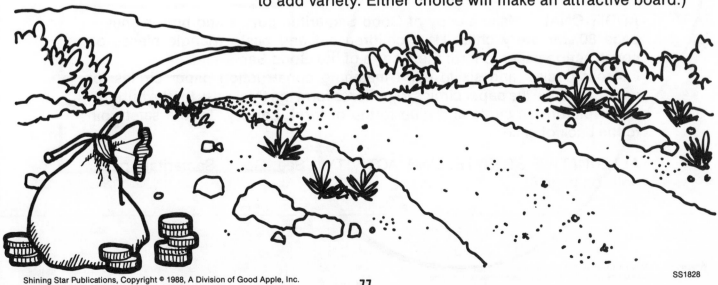

Shining Star Publications, Copyright © 1988, A Division of Good Apple, Inc.

SS1828

BE A GOOD SAMARITAN

GIVE A HELPING HAND

"... Go, and do thou likewise.   Luke 10:37

TABLE ACTIVITIES: Make a copy of the hand patterns, page 79, for each child. For a variety of color on the board, use different colors of fluorescent paper. Let each child cut out their own hand pattern. Have your class think of ways to be a Good Samaritan. Provide markers for children to write their own ideas on the paper hand. Smaller children might cut out appropriate magazine pictures and glue directly to paper hand. Arrange and staple hands onto board.

ADDITIONAL: Make a copy of Good Samaritan puzzle and button sheets, page 80, for every child. Have children cut and paste triangle pieces on construction paper to form the picture of the Good Samaritan.
Cut out circles, and six to eight matching construction paper circles for each one. Glue the paper circles together to form the thickness for the buttons. Color picture on circle and glue to top of form. Let dry. Tape a safety pin to the back of each.

ALTERNATIVE STORYTELLING ACTIVITY: See Good Samaritan paper dolls on page 81.

SS1828

GOOD SAMARITAN
(Bulletin Board Patterns)

GOOD SAMARITAN
(Puzzle and Button Patterns)

Circles for Good Samaritan buttons.

BE A GOOD SAMARITAN!

"...GO AND DO THOU LIKEWISE."

I LOVE YOU!

SS1828

GOOD SAMARITAN
Paper Dolls

Hang on donkey's back.

SS1828

LET THE CHILDREN COME

SS1828

Jesus was a very busy man. He traveled from city to city. He preached God's word and taught lessons to those who would listen. Jesus healed the sick who were brought to Him along the way.

Jesus was resting after a long day of teaching. Some small children were brought to Him, by their parents, to be blessed. The disciples knew Jesus was tired and told the people to take the children away.

But Jesus spoke up and stopped the disciples. Jesus said to let the children come to Him. He let the children know that He loved them. He gathered them around Him, and put His arms around them. Jesus enjoyed being with the children, and He wanted the disciples to know that it was good to spend time with children.

And as the disciples and all the people gathered there looked upon Jesus and the children, Jesus said to them, "The kingdom of God is for little children like these. And those of you who do not become like little children, will not enter the kingdom of God."

OBJECTIVE:
This bulletin board and table activities are designed to show the children how Jesus cared for them. He even told the adults in the story that in order for them to enter the kingdom of heaven they must become childlike. This lesson should make the children in your classroom feel very special.

PREPARATION:
Cover the background in a khaki burlap material. Reproduce drawing of Jesus on page 84. Use black or brown yarn to shape hair, mustache and beard. Staple or glue to burlap material. Use a scrap of solid-color material to make Jesus' robe and a contrasting color to drape across shoulder.

Have the children listen as you read Mark 10:13-16. Discuss how important and special each child is to Christ. Encourage the children to participate in the discussion. Have each one tell something special about themselves and then something special about a friend. Have each include talents God has blessed them with.

Also, include a discussion on what Jesus meant when He said that adults needed to be childlike to enter the kingdom of heaven. Point out that Christ was talking about positive childlike attributes, such as being obedient. We must all be obedient to our Lord!

LET THE CHILDREN COME

"... Suffer the little children to come unto me ...."

Mark 10:14

TABLE ACTIVITIES: Provide paper, pencils, crayons and markers for each child to draw a self-portrait. Color, cut out and staple the self-portraits around Jesus on the bulletin board. Give children pieces of yarn to connect from their self-portrait to Jesus' hand. This represents the bond between Jesus and children.

ADDITIONAL: Make a copy of the JESUS FLAG and the instructions on page 85 and 86 for each child. Each child will also need a dowel, crayons, scissors and paste or glue. Follow the instructions on page 85, and wave your flag for Jesus!

SS1828

LET THE CHILDREN COME
UNTO ME
(Bulletin Board Pattern)

SS1828

LET THE CHILDREN COME UNTO ME
(Flag Symbol Patterns)

Design your own JESUS flag!

1. Color the background of flag.

2. Choose one of the slogans provided, or write in a slogan of your own. Color, cut and paste in center of flag.

3. Choose any number of the symbols provided. Color, cut and paste onto flag.

4. Glue, tape or staple flag around dowel.

5. Wave your flag for JESUS!

SS1828

LET THE CHILDREN COME UNTO ME

(Flag Pattern)

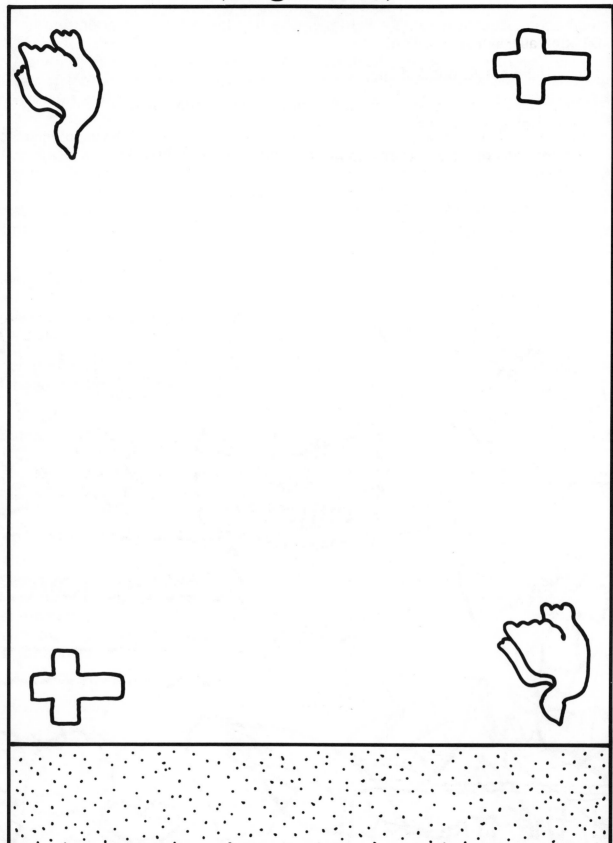

SS1828

ZACCHAEUS

On His journey Jesus passed through Jericho where crowds of people lined the road to see Him.

There was a man named Zacchaeus who wanted to see Jesus—the man he had heard so much about. Zacchaeus was a rich man who had taken from the poor, and he was looked upon as a sinner.

Because Zacchaeus was very short, he could not see over the crowds of people, so he climbed up into a sycamore tree. As Jesus came down the road, He looked up and saw Zacchaeus. He told Zacchaeus to come down so that He could be a guest in his house.

Zacchaeus was pleased. He hurried down the sycamore tree to take Jesus to his house. But when the crowds of people saw this, they began to whisper. Why was Jesus going to the house of a sinner?

Suddenly, Zacchaeus spoke to the Lord. He told Jesus he would give half of everything he owned to the poor. And to those he had taken from; he would return everything.

When the people heard Zacchaeus, they were amazed. And they heard Jesus forgive Zacchaeus and promise him salvation.

OBJECTIVE: In the story of Zacchaeus, the people wondered why Jesus wanted to spend time with a sinner. And yet as they watched, they saw a sinner saved and promised salvation. Jesus saves us all from our sins!

SKILL OBJECTIVE: A work sheet, on page 90, is provided for children to work with antonyms. (Antonyms are words that have opposite meanings.)

PREPARATION: Cover background with blue paper to represent sky. Enlarge pattern, on page 89, of Zacchaeus and tree trunk. Color with markers or crayons. Give each child a copy of a leaf to color, cut and paste onto board. Have the children arrange the leaves to form tree, but be sure to have Zacchaeus looking out from among the leaves. Cut letters out of colored construction paper and staple to board.

For a variation in the fall of the year, take your class on a nature walk to search for leaves for the bulletin board. If sycamore trees are available, choose the sycamore leaf in keeping with the story. However, any large, broad leaf would be attractive. And fall offers so many wonderful leaf colors to work with on your bulletin board.

"And he ran before, and climbed up into a sycamore tree to see him . . . ."
Luke 19:4

ZACCHAEUS

TABLE ACTIVITIES: Make a copy of the leaf, on page 89, for every child. Provide crayons, markers, scissors and paste so children can color, cut and paste the leaves to the board to form the tree.

ADDITIONAL: Discuss the definition of "antonym." (Antonyms are words that have opposite meanings.) Give examples: hot and cold, empty and full, big and little. Then, make a copy of the Antonym Sheet, on page 90, for each child. Explain the instructions. Have children cut and paste antonyms in the correct spaces. Then, color the pictures.

SS1828

ZACCHAEUS
(Bulletin Board Patterns)

SS1828

ZACCHAEUS

Antonym Sheet

Antonyms are words that are opposites. Choose the antonym that fits each sentence. Cut out and glue in the correct space.

Zacchaeus was a [tall] man.

Zacchaeus was [sad] to see Jesus.

Zacchaeus was a [fat] man.

Zacchaeus was [slow] coming down.

Zacchaeus climbed [down] the tree.

Zacchaeus stood [far from] Jesus.

[short]

[thin]

[fast]

[happy]

[up]

[near]

SS1828

HE IS RISEN

Jesus told His disciples that the day would come when He would be crucified on the cross. And indeed, all that He said did happen.

After His death, Jesus' body was placed in a tomb and a huge stone was rolled across the entrance.

Shortly thereafter, Mary Magdalene and Mary went to the tomb to take spices and oils to prepare Jesus' body for burial. But as they approached, they learned that a great earthquake had rolled the stone away from the entrance. And the angel of the Lord had come from heaven and sat upon the stone.

The angel spoke to the women and told them not to be afraid. The angel knew they had come to care for Jesus' body.

And the angel said, "He is not here: for he is risen." And the angel took the women inside the tomb so they could see Jesus' body was no longer there.

He instructed the women to go quickly and to tell the disciples that Jesus was risen from the dead. And they did as they were told, but on their way Jesus met them. And the women fell to their knees and worshipped the Lord.

OBJECTIVE:

Jesus showed total, unselfish love for all of us by dying on the cross. And as He arose from the dead, He saved us from our sins. We must praise God and be thankful for such a marvelous gift. Take time with your class to think of ways to thank our Lord.

Also, there is a DOVE AND CROSS MOBILE instruction sheet provided on page 94. Encourage the children to think of words that describe Christ's gift to us as He died on the cross for us. Examples: LOVE, LIFE, HOPE and PEACE. Make these words part of the mobile by writing them on the crosses.

PREPARATION:

Cover the background with bright yellow paper. Enlarge the crosses, page 93, on brown paper, or collage white paper with different colors of tissue paper for a stained-glass effect. Enlarge the dove, page 93, on white paper and cover with white feathers, if available. Or, cut two doves, glue around edges and stuff with newspaper to give a 3-D effect. Cut letters out of black construction paper and arrange on board.

HE IS RISEN

"He is not here: for he is risen . . . ."
Matthew 28:6

TABLE ACTIVITIES: Make a copy of the dove pattern and at least six of the small cross patterns, page 93, for each child. Provide crayons, scissors and yarn. Have the children color, cut and tie crosses to dove with yarn to make mobile. Write one word on each cross to represent Christ's gift to us through His death on the cross and resurrection. (Examples: LOVE, PEACE, HOPE and FORGIVENESS)

ADDITIONAL: Hand out a copy of the JESUS CHRIST—EASTER CARD, pages 95 and 96, to each child. Provide crayons, scissors and paste.

Discuss, plan and carry out an Adopt-a-Grandparent program for your class. See instructions on page 95.

SS1828

HE IS RISEN
(Bulletin Board and Table Activity Patterns)

HE IS RISEN
(Mobile Pattern)

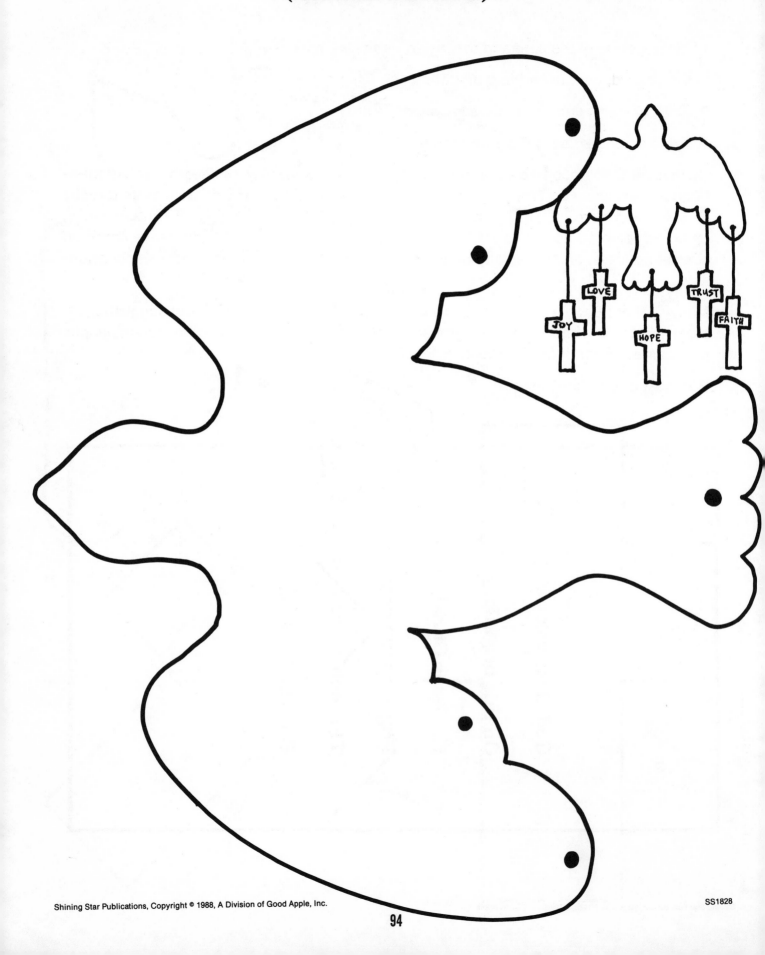

SS1828

HE IS RISEN
(Easter Card Pattern)

1. Make copies of the card and the inside verse for each child.

2. Color card, cut out and fold on dotted line.

3. Cut out insert and paste message inside card.

4. Send card to an adopted grandparent.

SUGGESTION: Encourage the children to share their love by developing an Adopt-a-Grandparent program. You may obtain a list of names through any church, or go directly to a nursing home. Contact the "grandparent" first and ask if they are interested in being adopted so as not to infringe on their privacy. Send the grandparent's cards on special holidays, and especially on their birthdays. Make phone calls and visit occasionally.

Many of these people are lonely and will welcome visits by children. Other suggestions—bake goodies and share, help buy groceries, run errands, introduce to other caring people, play games of dominos, checkers, etc.

But most of all, show respect!

God bless us now
On this bright day.
For Jesus Christ has
Prepared the way
Through heaven's door
For which we pray.
Amen

HE IS RISEN
(Easter Card Pattern)

Jesus

Christ

SS1828